The Right Measures

The Story of a Company's Journey to Find the True Indicators of Its Success and Values

Mark A. Nash and Sheila R. Poling

CRC Press
Taylor & Francis Group
Boca Raton   London   New York

CRC Press is an imprint of the
Taylor & Francis Group, an **informa** business

A PRODUCTIVITY PRESS BOOK

CRC Press
Taylor & Francis Group
6000 Broken Sound Parkway NW, Suite 300
Boca Raton, FL 33487-2742

© 2013 by Taylor & Francis Group, LLC
CRC Press is an imprint of Taylor & Francis Group, an Informa business

---

Library of Congress Cataloging-in-Publication Data

Nash, Mark A., 1959-
    The right measures : the story of a company's journey to find the true indicators of its success and values / Mark A. Nash, Sheila R. Poling.
        p. cm. -- (Routledge companions in business, management, and accounting)
    Includes index.
    ISBN 978-1-4398-7865-1 (pbk.)
    1. Management. 2. Organizational behavior. 3. Organizational change. I. Poling, Sheila R. II. Title.

HD30.4.N37 2012
658--dc23   2012017234

Visit the Taylor & Francis Web site at
http://www.taylorandfrancis.com

and the CRC Press Web site at
http://www.crcpress.com

The Right Measures

Measures

The Story of a Company's Journey to
Find the True Indicators of Its
Success and Values

In memory of two teachers in my life:
Maxine Housholder, who first inspired me to write;
Liz Burdette, who taught me to get the facts and tell the story.
And, of course, my appreciation is always with my wife, Staci,
and my daughters for allowing me the time to write this tale.

—Mark A. Nash

Dr. W. Edwards Deming always said to find
"Joy in Work."
Pearl S. Buck said,
"To find joy in work is to discover the fountain of youth."
I am so blessed to have found joy in my work. Thank you to
those I work with (coworkers, customers, and publishers) who
contribute to this joy on a daily basis. Keep up the good work!!

—Sheila R. Poling

Contents

Prologue

In today's fast-paced global economy, all organizations are feeling the pressure to perform at a much higher level and much faster than ever before. The problem that exists for many organizations is that to achieve this operational speed, some processes do not receive the attention they truly require, or worse, they are ignored.

For many companies, measuring how the organization is operating, beyond looking at the top and/or bottom line, is way too often the biggest casualty. This may be the first victim of our *always connected* business world for smaller organizations, but large corporations can also fall victim to this problem.

It is true that there are companies today that are well aware of this possibility and work extremely hard to *not* fall into the trap of ignoring the process of measuring success and failure. Unfortunately, it is also possible to overact and measure too much. And when an organization overmeasures, you quite often get the same results as when you do not measure at all: a lack of understanding, focus, and direction.

Organizational measures are the foundational building blocks for success. In order for all employees of an organization (not just managers) to understand what is important and how the individual impacts the overall organizational goals and objectives, there must be a structured measurement system in place from the bottom of the organization to the top. At the lowest level, employees use measures to understand how they are performing as individuals. The measures used to show employees' success must tie into the measures used to show team success. And as you climb higher in the organization, each level shown must tie into the level above until you have your measures linked to your key performance indicators (KPIs) at the top of the organization.

But just creating a system of measures is not the answer. You *must* measure the right things. **The things you measure are a reflection of your organizational values. And these values are the fundamental**

building blocks that shape your organization's vision and action. When you think about the preceding statement, consider:

If you are not measuring, then what is your vision? What actions should you be taking? If you are not measuring the right things, then how can you achieve your vision? And, if you measure everything, how do you provide proper focus toward your vision?

You measure what you value. Measures directly influence how people work. In turn, how people work affects organizational results (top-line growth, bottom-line profitability, and increased customer satisfaction). To engage your workforce to effectively improve the desired results of the organization, you must have a measurement system that each employee understands. They must be involved and have ownership in that system. To accomplish this, you must have a strategy of engagement, not of implementation where managers and engineers have a list of things to measure and go forth and gather, analyze, and post. You must create a system where the employees help develop what you measure so that it has value to them and the organization.

The story you are about to read is not about a company that does not measure—quite the opposite. This tale is about a company, M.E. Burdette Co., that overmeasures. It is the story of a high-end storage container manufacturing company that manufactures storage containers for a variety of industries. In their quest to make sure that every area of the organization succeeds, they have put in place a metrics system that measures in great detail how each department and team is doing against their individual goals and objectives. Quite often, these goals are arbitrary or capricious, established by managers as a way to show incremental success without regard to the rest of the organization. By doing this, each of the departments may be optimized, but the overall organization may be suboptimized and the goals and objectives will not be achieved. Our hope is that you will see this company's journey of discovery about the value of measures and how to establish a system that involves the entire organization.

Chapter 1

A New Job

September 8

"Wake up, Narvell!"

Narvell opened his eyes and looked around. Had someone really shouted at him or had he been dreaming? As he searched the faces in the room, it appeared as though no one was looking at him, so Narvell straightened himself in the chair and hoped it had just been a dream. But *was* this meeting a dream? Or was his new career choice turning out to be one really bad and boring, not to mention confusing, reality?

Narvell T. Mann had been sitting in the corporate conference center now for more than four hours. He had listened, or mostly listened, to three different vice presidents and two directors explain to him and the other twenty-six people in the room about the financial health of the company. Narvell's boss, the director of engineering, was now going into great detail about numerous engineering projects. He appeared to be well equipped with enough charts, graphs, and data to make any engineer proud. After another twenty minutes of long-winded and quite detailed answers that Narvell thought to be mainly hot air, his new boss, Bill Cooke, finally came to a close. Looking around the room, Bill asked, "Does anyone have any questions?" Then, not really waiting for anyone to raise their hand, or open their mouth, Bill continued, "Great. Mr. Schmidt, I believe that's all we have for you today." With that, Bill took his seat on the front row of the conference center.

As Fred Schmidt, the CEO of M.E. Burdette Co., came to the podium, Narvell begin to think about this first big meeting. He realized that he knew very little about the company where he had just come to work, and had learned nothing from today's experience. Panic began to set in as Narvell quietly beat himself up for not understanding anything that had been presented during the previous four hours. Thinking to himself, he asked, "What am I doing here? Why was I invited to this meeting? Am I stupid? What am I missing?" Just then, Mr. Schmidt began to speak, snapping Narvell back to reality.

"Now, if someone would like to explain to me what in the world is going on, maybe we can get somewhere. Each and every one of you who presented this morning gave us a very detailed explanation of what is going on in your area. Yet, I still have no more idea about why we're losing money than I did when the meeting started. Sales claims they are making their goals. Manufacturing is saying the same thing about meeting the production schedule. Purchasing showed us data that supports their primary objective of the year to lower the cost of purchased materials by 3.5%. And now, Engineering tells us we are on target on all but one project. So, if everyone of you is doing so well this year, why are we not making any money?" Narvell sat there dumbfounded at what he had just heard come out of the mouth of their CEO.

Mr. Schmidt continued, "I want Bill, Dane, and Allyson to review this entire packet of information and see what, if anything, can be used to help us turn this situation around."

After sitting through four hours of nothing but charts, graphs, explanations, excuses, and finger pointing, Narvell was suddenly beginning to wonder if he had made the right choice in accepting this position. On the job for just under three weeks, he still felt like a fish out of water. He took this job as a cost analyst expecting to learn a great deal about engineering, manufacturing, costing, and corporate management. And now, here he was sitting in a meeting listening to the president ask the same questions he was thinking. Of course, Narvell hadn't known the company was losing money at the beginning of the day. Now he did, and he was beginning to worry.

He began to reflect on his life since joining the company. In his short time here, he had learned very little, if anything at all, about the company. His first day on the job, he had been given a stack of reports to read. When he finished reading through the reports, he went to his new boss, Bill Cooke, and asked what he should do next. Bill's response was simple and somewhat short, "I'm too busy to get with you right now. I'll have one of the engineers get with you after lunch." After lunch never came, and he wound up sitting around for several days doing nothing. Narvell finally took it upon himself to ask one of the friendlier engineers, Jimbo Chisholm, if he had anything he could do. Jimbo told him to grab a notepad and join him in

Conference Room C. For the next two weeks, Narvell had shadowed Jimbo's team working on a project for one of M.E. Burdette Co.'s largest customers. During that entire time, not only did he never receive any instruction from Bill, he never saw him. And now, here he was sitting in the corporate conference center totally confused and wondering if he had made the biggest mistake of his life.

Mr. Schmidt's continued monologue caught Narvell's attention once more. "The board of directors has stated very clearly that they want to know why profits are down and why we're losing market share. I called this meeting expecting someone to give me something I could tell to the board. However, what I heard contradicts the financials and the board's feelings. Does anyone have anything I can take back to the board?" When no one responded, Mr. Schmidt picked up his notebook and walked out of the room. Apparently, this meeting was over.

Just as Narvell started to get up out of his chair, Jimbo leaned over and said, "Welcome to M.E. Burdette Co." He then quickly stood up and headed out of the room. Narvell quickly caught up with Jimbo and they headed down the hall towards Engineering. Narvell asked Jimbo, "What was that meeting all about? What did Mr. Schmidt mean about not learning anything? Wasn't that good information? And by the way, why the heck was I even invited to this meeting? I'm just a cost analyst. I'm not even an engineer, much less a manager or director."

Jimbo replied without thinking or even really hesitating. "The entire engineering staff goes to every one of these goals and objectives update meetings. No questions asked. Mr. Schmidt requires it. And just like every other meeting, we usually leave the meeting with more questions than answers."

"Why?" asked Narvell looking around as if he expected someone else to walk up and answer the question.

"Why do we all go? Or why do we always leave with more questions than answers?" asked Jimbo.

"Both," responded Narvell, with a bit of agitation now in his voice. "If we are the biggest manufacturing company in town, and we have the biggest market share in our industry, why is everyone so confused about what's going on?"

"Look, Narvell, I don't pretend to understand what goes on with anything in this company except in my little corner of Engineering. What I do know is that no one in our department questions the big dogs upstairs. If you do, Bill will make sure you aren't around to ask a second question."

"Bill?" asked Narvell, beginning to feel confused again.

"Your boss, Bill Cooke. You remember him?"

"Jimbo, you say that as if someone is hiding something. Why can no one ask questions?" Narvell was beginning to really doubt his career decision now.

"Okay, I'll say this one more time and hopefully this will be simple enough to get through that thick head of yours. Don't ask questions about our metrics. Apparently, Bill and his buddies upstairs are very proud of the way we report success, and I suppose the way they explain the occasional failure. It doesn't seem to really matter if you, me, anyone else in Engineering, or even anyone on the manufacturing floor can understand the big picture from these charts and graphs that get posted on the wall. It doesn't matter how many people read or don't read the wall of lame ... uh .... I did not just say that .... What is important is that all of the different areas are meeting their goals. They'll all get together tomorrow and create a report for Mr. Schmidt and his vice presidents to deliver to the board. Then the world will be great for another ninety days or so." And with that one last comment, Jimbo slipped into his office leaving Narvell standing alone in the hall.

As he headed back to his cubicle in the Engineering department's maze of partitions, Narvell tried to replay the entire meeting in his mind. With each bit of information he could recall, he tried to tie it to something, anything for that matter, which he could remember from his research about M.E. Burdette Co. and his job interviews when he was searching for a job. Something didn't add up here, yet Narvell couldn't quite put his finger on it.

Sitting down at his cubicle desk, Narvell woke his computer up and logged into the network. Without really thinking about it, he navigated his way through the list of virtual drives and opened the Y: drive where the company metrics were housed. Each division of the company had its own folder. Within each folder were subfolders for each department. In these department folders were the tables and charts that numerous managers, directors, and vice presidents had reported on earlier, and, apparently, their careers hung on the results that were kept in these folders. Narvell started to look through the folder labeled Finance. When he opened the folder, he saw subfolders for Accounts Payable, Accounts Receivable, Benefits Administration, Budget, Financial Analysis, Payroll, and Warranty Service. Narvell double-clicked on Accounts Payable and was immediately met with a pop-up window that informed him he did not have authorization to access the folder. He repeated this for each of the other folders and was met with the exact same message. "So much for that idea," thought Narvell as he hit the **Back** button and returned to the root directory of the Y: drive and clicked into the folder marked Engineering. "Okay, let's see what our own department has to say."

Narvell wasn't sure if he was shocked, stunned, or frustrated at what happened next. The Engineering folder opened and it was empty. No sub-folders; no files; nothing. Narvell sat and stared at the computer screen for several minutes in silence. When he finally regained his thoughts from what was in front of him, or more correctly, what was not in front of him, he returned to the root directory and quickly opened the Manufacturing folder. This time he found a long list of subfolders; one for each work center on the manufacturing floor. Problem was, just like Finance, he couldn't open a single subfolder. Same problem existed when he tried to look through Sales and Marketing; and, then again, when he took a shot at both Facilities and Quality Assurance.

Narvell finally thought he had found some data to answer his curios-ity when he opened the Human Resources folder. There were only three subfolders located here. Narvell double-clicked to open the first folder titled Environmental. It opened in a new window and a single file was sitting in this subfolder. Half expecting a message to pop up saying the file was not accessible, Narvell clicked on the file, and it opened. What he saw prompted a guttural sound much like getting hit in the stomach, that in hindsight, Narvell was sure could be heard throughout the department. The screen in front of him simply said:

TO VIEW THIS METRIC, SEE THE **EMPLOYEE INFORMATION BOARD** OUTSIDE THE MAIN BREAK ROOM IN MANUFACTURING

Narvell backed up in the network again and opened the subfolder called HR. Once again, he found a single file, and when opened, had the exact same message. Without even bothering to go into the Safety subfolder, Narvell closed his browser and tossed his cordless mouse into the far corner of the desk. He leaned back and stared at the framed poster with the single word *Teamwork* on the wall outside his cubicle.

"Yeah, right. Teamwork. Where? Not in this company," Narvell said quietly.

All he was trying to do was understand a single management meeting that included every upper-level manager in the company plus the entire engineering team. What makes this company tick? Where did the reports that were presented come from? How does an employee review this information and gain knowledge? And the one person Narvell felt comfortable with in asking about what was going on had already told him *not to ask questions*!

"Well, I guess I'll head out to the break room," Narvell announced as he stood up. Then he realized that no one was listening, or probably even cared, and he began to feel a little bit silly.

***

Narvell appeared in front of the giant metrics board, which consisted of an entire wall outside the main manufacturing break room just as the afternoon bell sounded announcing the end of the afternoon break. He stood and looked over this incredibly large wall of information, nearly six feet tall by more than fifteen feet wide, while the production employees streamed by on their way back to the manufacturing floor. As the last employee slowly walked past him, it occurred to Narvell that not one person seemed to look at the wall or him as they had passed by. It was almost as if he and the metrics board were invisible. Walking to the left side of the board, Narvell began to study the data in front of him. The wall was divided into sections; one each for the various divisions of the company. Much of the information he had heard this morning was posted here. The Sales division was the subject of the first column. The tables and graphs here appeared to be very thorough: Actual Total Sales; Revenue versus Forecast; Actual Sales by Region versus Forecast; Margin versus Goal for Past 12 Months; Margin by Region versus Goal for Past 12 Months; # of New Accounts by Region; # of New Contacts by Sales Rep—the charts and graphs went on and on. Narvell counted twenty different metrics for Sales.

Moving over to look at the Manufacturing Team, as they called themselves, Narvell was even more impressed. There were charts showing the number of jobs produced by month, week, and day; charts showing number and percentage of jobs completed on time; graphs showing the breakdown of parts produced by product family, top ten parts by quantity; productivity tables for each manufacturing cell on the floor, as well as a table showing the productivity rating for each employee; and, scrap and defect charts by part, manufacturing cell, and supplier. Narvell began to realize just how much data was being tracked throughout the company, and he was barely halfway through the second set of metrics posted on the wall.

After stopping his count in the manufacturing section at forty-seven different sets of data, Narvell thought he would take a look at Engineering. A sense of pride began to creep over Narvell as he looked at the engineering department's set of metrics. There was a graph showing number of projects started by month with a bold red line showing the goal per month; a chart showing hours worked per project versus budget; and, a chart showing how each project was progressing against milestone dates. Each of these charts and graphs showed just how well the department was doing against the goals that had been set for them. Narvell then noticed that there was a series of charts showing the number of products that had been modified. These charts showed the number of product revisions by month, hours put into the revisions, and expected cost savings from changes and/or improved margins.

"This is good stuff," Narvell said quietly to himself as he continued to look through the remaining metrics on the board for Engineering. After studying the remaining data for his own department, Narvell spent the next forty-five minutes going over the Quality Assurance, Human Resources, Finance, and finally, Marketing's metrics. Narvell looked down at his watch and realized he had just spent the entire afternoon, nearly two and a half hours, reviewing the information on this wall.

As he stood there in front of the massively detailed wall of measurements, Narvell began to think about what Mr. Schmidt had said at the meeting this morning. So, why did he not know the answers to his questions? It appeared that there was more than enough data here to run the company. Why was the M.E. Burdette Co. losing money? Narvell rescanned the charts for Sales, Marketing, and Manufacturing. If everyone was hitting their goals as these charts showed, then what was the problem?

Pulling his smartphone out of its holder on his belt, Narvell began to take pictures of the wall. Breaking it down by division, Narvell shot three or four photos of each section. He really didn't know why he did this; it just seemed like the right thing to do. Perhaps he would have a brilliant thought in the middle of the night, review the data in the photos, and then answer all of his questions, and maybe Mr. Schmidt's as well.

***

Sitting down at his desk, Narvell woke up his personal computer and checked his e-mail. Looking at his inbox, Narvell saw yet another e-mail from Chris Anselmo. Chris had been Narvell's roommate his junior year in college, and as Narvell recalled, it had not been a very pleasant experience. Thankfully, Chris had been a senior, took a job with his family's company, and moved out of the apartment the day he had graduated. This e-mail was nearly identical to the other seven or eight e-mails Chris had sent him.

Whatever it was that Chris wanted, Narvell wasn't really interested. After all, he had bigger fish to fry at this point in his young career, didn't he? And with that simple thought, Narvell decided that he was going to solve the big mystery that Mr. Schmidt had laid out in the meeting that morning.

| Delete | Reply | ▼ | Forward | ⇩ ⇧ | Spam | Move | ▼ | Print | Actions | ▼ |

I'm in Town
　　From: Chris.Anselmo
　　　To: Narvell.Mann

Add to Contacts

Narv-

I'm in town working and want to get together. I hope this is the right email address.

Chris

Opening his web browser, Narvell navigated to his online blog. To him, a safe place where he could document his thoughts, twenty-four hours a day. Locked down as private, only those individuals that he gave access to could see his innermost thoughts. And in the three years he had been blogging, Narvell had not once allowed anyone else in. He quickly started a new entry. He *would* figure this metrics thing out at M.E. Burdette Co.

What's Happening at M.E. Burdette Co.?

Posted on **September 8, 2011**
Reply

- M.E. Burdette Co. losing money?
- How much money?
- Sales is hitting their goals.
- Engineering is ahead of most milestones on both new and improved products.
- Manufacturing is beating the pants off their goals
- Every division is within budget except Transportation, most likely due to the rising price of fuel …….. AGAIN!
  S.O. W.I.L.L. S.O.M.E.O.N.E. P.L.E.A.S.E. T.E.L.L. M.E. W.H.Y. I T.O.O.K. T.H.I.S. J.O.B.???????????

Posted in Blogs from the book | Leave a reply

With this first entry complete, or as complete as it was going to get this evening anyway, Narvell shut down his computer and headed for the parking lot after what suddenly seemed like a very long day.

Chapter 2

What a Day!

Narvell pulled in the driveway at home and noticed that his roommate, Bobby Evans, was already home. Bobby was a nice enough guy, not real bright, but easy enough to live with. Narvell had met him working in an electronics manufacturer's distribution center just before his senior year in college. Bobby was one of those guys who were on the seven-year plan at the university, and it didn't look like he would ever finish college. The night Narvell accepted the job at M.E. Burdette Co., he had run into Bobby at a bar just off campus, where he had stopped for a celebratory drink after accepting the position with M.E. Burdette at the close of his third interview. As they drank the night away, Narvell mentioned that he was now going to have to find a place to live since he was back in town to stay. Bobby spoke right out saying that his roommate moved out the week before, and he was welcome to room with him. That was that. After graduating, Narvell had moved home to commence his career search only to wind up back in this neighborhood just off campus. It wasn't a bad house … sort of like what you'd expect with a couple of young, single guys in the college town.

And so, for the past month Narvell had been trying to get used to living with Bobby—a bit of a goofball and a minor slob, but all in all he was not a bad roommate. Walking through the door, Narvell noticed that Bobby was actually cleaning the living room. "What the heck are you doing, Bobby?" Narvell asked as he came through the door and threw his keys on the table by the television.

"Cleaning up. What does it look like?"

"I know you're cleaning up. Why?"

"We have company coming over. I ran into an old friend of ours and I thought it might be fun to just hang out and have a few beers and remember our college days," Bobby said as he swept some paper, bits of popcorn, and a few beer bottles off of the couch and into the trashcan he was holding.

"First of all Bobby, our college days were only five months ago. Second, last time I looked, you were still in college. And third, who is it?"

"I'm not telling. It's a surprise. Now go in there and see if we have anything to eat, and if not, call and order a pizza. I'll pay. Now move it. He'll be here any minute," said Bobby as he headed for his bedroom.

"Great. Just what I need. After a day like today, I don't need any more surprises," Narvell said to himself as he picked up the phone to call and order the pizza.

After ordering dinner, Narvell headed for his room to change clothes and grab a couple of minutes of solitude before Bobby's mystery guest showed up. He changed into a pair of shorts and a T-shirt and then collapsed on the bed. But luck was not on Narvell's side this day, and as soon as he closed his eyes, the doorbell rang. Bobby yelled from the other end of the house and even though his voice was muffled, it was obvious that he wanted Narvell to open the door. The bed felt good beneath his aching body, and so Narvell just continued to lie on his bed ignoring Bobby's muted pleas. Finally, footsteps could be heard in the front of the house and Narvell decided he wasn't going to be able to avoid this evening that he was not looking forward to.

Getting up off the bed, Narvell slowly opened his door and stepped out into the hall. Before he was even in the living room, he could hear a familiar voice and a huge lump appeared in his throat. He knew that voice, and he immediately realized that he was about to spend the evening with the two people he had once assumed he would never see again after graduating from college. Sure enough, walking into the living room, Narvell was standing face to face with the one and only, Chris Anselmo.

Chris came across the room in what seemed to Narvell like a single, very large step. He grabbed Narvell in one sweeping motion and gave him a bear hug that nearly choked the life out of the startled, and now quite out of breath, Narvell. After what Narvell imagined to be a thirty-minute hug, Chris finally put him down and stepped back. "Narv, my man, you look great. How long has it been?"

"Chris, you're as bad as Bobby. It's only been like a year and a half. You guys act like it's been decades since we've seen each other. I saw your email this afternoon at work. It was one wild day. Sorry I didn't reply. So what brings you back to town anyway?"

"Well, you know I took a job at Housholder Sprockets right? And you do know that my grandfather started the company and demands that every family member that wants to work for the company gets to start at the bottom. I was fortunate enough to start working summers back when I was in high school. But it didn't stop our management team from sending me to the hinterlands to work in one of our hottest and most chaotic facilities. After spending four months at our plant down on the border, I got a call that I had been selected, and not by my father or grandfather mind you, to participate in our management training and mentoring program here at the main plant and in the corporate office. So, here I am. And you … hum, let's see. You hunted for a job for four months and finally settled for a position at M.E. Burdette right down the road from where we all met, right?"

"Yeah, something like that. But I'll tell you this, after today, I'm not sure I made the right decision. I just had one twisted, confusing day at the plant. If this is the way this company is run, I'm not so sure I have much of a future here," Narvell explained as he slumped down into the very worn out, old leather recliner.

Just then, the doorbell rang announcing that dinner was here. Narvell gladly allowed the interruption to shift the conversation away from his problem. Bobby ran off to the kitchen and came back with an ice chest full of beer. Just like Bobby, bringing in an ice chest full of beer when the refrigerator is only fifteen feet away. Small talk consumed the time between bites of pizza and swigs from their bottles of beer.

After finishing off two large pizza supremes and two beers each, of course Bobby had five, but no one was counting, Chris turned the conversation back to Narvell's comments about bad decisions. "Why do you think you made a bad career choice Narvell? What in the world could have happened during your first month on the job to make you think about bailing out so soon?"

Narvell summarized his meeting and the odd interaction Mr. Schmidt had had with the management team and engineers. "But I really don't understand what is going on. I went down to the break room on the manufacturing floor this afternoon and looked at the metrics on our wall. There were like over one hundred different measurements on the wall, and when you go through them, you see how well each department is doing. So why are we losing money? What am I missing in all this? And why do I have such an uneasy feeling about my own boss?"

Without missing a beat, Bobby sat up on the edge of the couch where he had been lying, and without waiting to see if Chris was going to say anything, Bobby blurted out in a not-so-soft voice, "That boss of yours is a crook. If he gets rid of people who question his numbers, he's got to be hiding something. I bet he's stealing from the company!" And with that, Bobby fell over backwards onto the sofa and was fast asleep.

Narvell looked at Chris with an inquisitive expression on his face. "Do you think there might be something going on? That's a hell of a way to start out a career, working with criminals. Oh man, am I going to wind up in jail?" Narvell laughed nervously as he thought about what he had just said. "Chris, all companies can't be this screwed up, can they? What's it like at Housholder? How do you all measure your business?"

"Wow. Big questions, Narvell. I don't know that I can easily answer that. But, if you'll get us both another beer, I'll give it a shot."

Narvell got up and walked to the far end of the sofa where Bobby was sleeping, reached in the ice chest, and pulled out two more cold ones. As Narvell popped the tops on the beers, Chris began explaining business at Housholder Sprockets.

"From day one, my grandfather has tried to keep the way we measure and monitor our successes and failures as simple as possible. Over the years, the company has always looked at just a few basic metrics to measure success. Well, what I should really say is at the top of the company, my grandfather's executive team uses just a few key performance indicators, or KPIs, to *see* what is happening. And he pushes that philosophy throughout the company. My father says granddad is a bit overbearing about it. But, hey, it works.

"Every time we hire or promote someone into management, they get the honor of spending a solid week with granddad observing how he runs the company. Then they have to meet with him once a month for a year. These meetings are nothing but reviews and reminders of where we came from as a company, where we are, and where we are going. Or so I've been told. I haven't been anointed yet. After I go through this training program, I'll have to do it, too. There is one thing that granddad always asks each manager, and I'm going to ask you the same question when we get through talking about Housholder—but, not yet.

"Something you should understand about Housholder is that you probably won't find many other companies our size with the moral and ethical integrity that we have. I'm not saying we're perfect, but I can say that it is preached throughout the company that managers will deal swiftly with moral or ethical problems. Dad had to fire a lifelong friend for lying. The guy had worked for the company for fifteen years. He got caught in a lie and when he admitted it, he knew the consequences. My dad knew the consequences. If he hadn't fired him, granddad would have fired them both. And it wasn't because dad is just a son-in-law. I think granddad would fire my uncle Dave if he didn't deal with an ethical issue properly. Can you believe that? Fire your own son? But hey, it has made us the company we are today. And I can tell you that the vast majority of our employees are thrilled we are as upright a company as we are."

Bobby rolled over on the couch and mumbled a bit in his sleep. Both Narvell and Chris looked at him, and it was fairly obvious that Narvell's roommate would not be participating in any more of this conversation tonight.

Chris looked at Narvell and turned the conversation back to the problems Narvell had described at M.E. Burdette. "Explain to me again what you witnessed this morning and then let's go over the numbers you saw on the … what did you call it? The wall of lame?"

"No. I said that's what I heard Jimbo call it. His comments have really turned my thoughts upside down. The meeting this morning was just one director or VP after another explaining all the great and wonderful things their areas were accomplishing and showing charts and graphs to back up their statements. The metrics board by the main break room seemed to back up everything they said. What I don't understand is how you can have over a hundred different measurements on the wall, and yet, I could find nothing on the network server to substantiate any of it. And then Mr. Schmidt's very pointed question seemed to faze no one but me. I don't even know where to start. What metric or metrics should I be looking at first? Where do I dig to find out what is going on?"

And suddenly Narvell had an uneasy feeling start to grow in the pit of his stomach. He started to think over everything he had just told Chris, and he began to wonder if he had said too much. Was it right to be comparing notes about how companies operate with the competition? Well really not the competition, Narvell thought, but sort of. After all, the university was the largest employer in town, the school district was second, M.E. Burdette was third, and then came Housholder Sprockets. This was the company that was said to always be stealing employees from M.E. Burdette. Narvell was beginning to fall down that rabbit hole trying to reconcile the things he had heard at work with the statements from Chris about being so ethical, when Chris brought him back to the present one more time.

"Okay, Narv. Let's say something bad is going on at Burdette … what can you do about it? What if nothing is going on? What then? Have you even considered what you might be doing to a promising career if you go plowing through the company like a bull in a china shop looking for some dastardly deeds that may not even exist? Dude, get a grip. If you really want to help, do a little analysis work, find out what you can that does make sense. And let me ask you that question I mentioned earlier. *What's your tape measure?*"

"It's out in the toolbox in the garage. What do you need my tape measure for?" asked Narvell, quite confused at this seemingly off-the-wall request.

"Not, where's your tape measure, what's your tape measure? That's what my grandfather asks every single person who goes to work for us in management. What is your tape measure?" responded Chris, now with a bit of excitement in his voice.

"What the heck are you talking about? Why do you want to know what my tape measure is? What does a tape measure at Housholder Sprockets have to do with the financial problems at my company? All I'm trying to do is figure out what the heck is going on and I thought you might be able to help. Well, thanks for nothing!" Narvell fired off in rapid-fire succession, raising his voice to show his displeasure at this strange turn of events in their conversation.

Chris responded to this outburst in a calm tone that immediately defused the tension. "Whoa, big guy. Calm down. I'm trying to help. My grandfather's philosophy seems to have worked for years and our management team works great together. They truly are a team. Ask any one of them, and they will tell you that the one question granddad asks them about their tape measure is what starts the journey within our company. I'm no expert on the subject, but I have listened to my father and grandfather discuss it at length time and time again when our family gets together. I'm sure they do the same thing at work. Your whole story sounds exactly like many of the tales I've heard granddad tell dad over the years about new managers with plenty of experience coming into our company. Some of the stories they've told granddad get told over and over again as dad and granddad analyze what other companies do. If you want to figure this all out, I'll help you. But, you have to get a firm foundation under you first. Humor me just a little and answer the question. What's your tape measure?"

"Okay, Chris. I still am not sure what you're talking about. But, I'll play your silly game. What's my tape measure? I don't know. I have no idea what that means. But, I want to figure this out. So, what do I do? Where do I go from here? If you aren't talking about the tape measure in my garage, I'm at a dead end. Help me out, Chris. I'm throwing you my lifeline. Please grab it and pull me in." And with that last comment, Narvell began to laugh, not just at what he had said, but at the absurdity of the whole situation.

"You've got to start by gathering data that might help answer my question. Actually, you already have some data. But I don't think it's necessarily the right data. The answer isn't there yet. I want you to go to work and dive deep. Try understanding what makes the company run," Chris said before being interrupted by Narvell.

"But I …, " began Narvell, only to be cut off quickly by Chris.

"Let me finish, Narvell. Don't respond to what I say, just listen. Go back to work and try to figure out what makes the company tick. What is it that makes Burdette successful? How do employees know you are successful? How does management know you are successful? How do the stockholders know you are successful? Don't answer, just go back and find the answers. Document what you find when you find it. Don't wait. You still blog?"

At that question, Narvell nodded an affirmative, rather weakly.

"Jot down the info in your blog. I assume it's still private. You haven't gotten the courage up yet to share it with the world, right?"

Again, Narvell nodded.

"We can meet for pizza or burgers again in a week or so. How about next Friday or Saturday and we can discuss what you've learned? If you run into any brick walls while you are searching, I'll give you a tip. Call the Bean. I bet she can help you out."

"The Bean?" Narvell replied. "Does Annie work at Burdette?"

"I thought you knew that, Narvell. Obviously you haven't run into her yet."

"No. You really think she'd help me find out what is going on?"

"Of course she will. All you have to do is ask," replied Chris as he got up from his seat and headed for the door. "I've got to run … long day again tomorrow. I get the pleasure of starting my management training this week … five straight days of classes and workshops. See ya."

And with that, Chris was out the door and Narvell was standing alone in the living room. Well, not quite alone, since Bobby was sprawled out on the couch, and was now snoring. With that, Narvell locked the front door, turned out the lights, and headed back to his bedroom.

Sitting down in front of his computer, Narvell logged in to his blog page and began to write. As tired as he was, he knew he must get the conversation with Chris down before he forgot all of it.

After rereading the blog entry twice to make sure it sounded right, Narvell logged out. Going over to his bed, he collapsed on it without bothering to change his clothes or turn out the lights.

What a Day!

Posted on **September 8, 2011**
Reply

What a day! First my head spins after sitting through my first management update meeting. Then I come home to an impromptu party and wind up revisiting my day in total.

I still have no clue why M.E. Burdette Co. is losing money! Nothing has changed in five hours. However, after visiting with a former roommate at an apparently very successful company here in town, I am challenged, if not still frustrated, to find out what is going on at Burdette.

In order to figure this thing out, I have been told by Chris Anselmo to find my tape measure. Actually he said "What is your tape measure." In order to solve the mystery, I need to:

- Figure out what my tape measure is. Is this mine, or is it M.E. Burdette's tape measure?
- Start to unravel the mystery of the loss at Burdette by understanding the way we run the company.
- DON'T JUMP TO CONCLUSIONS!!!!!!!!!!!!
- Get as much data as I can to help in this INVESTIGATION.
- Call the Bean, if I need help.

Sounds so simple when I write it down on paper. But why is it so frustrating? Why is the answer not there? And what can Annie Gerdes, AKA the Bean, do to help. I don't even know what department she works in.

Tomorrow I must look back through all the info I saw today and see what is missing. There was lots of good data on the board by the break room. I think we shall start the investigation there.

Posted in Blogs from the book | Leave a reply

Chapter 3

More Questions Than Answers

September 9

Narvell walked into the office the next day with a new sense of direction. He actually was in a very good position to continue his investigation into the troubles at M.E. Burdette since Bill Cooke, his boss, had still never given him an assignment. He found this odd, but it gave him plenty of time to search for answers. The question was where to start? How should he go about finding out what was going on? What had the CEO of this company been so upset and frustrated about?

Slipping into his cubicle, Narvell logged into his computer and once again headed to the network drive that was identified as housing the company's metrics. He very methodically went through each folder one at a time, drilling down into all of the subfolders to see if he could find any more information than he had found yesterday. After nearly an hour of searching, he opened a folder underneath Sales named Outside Sales—Northeast Region. In this folder, he found a single spreadsheet file titled Metrics.

When he double-clicked on the file, he was surprised that not only did it open without a password, but, it actually contained data. Just as he started to read what was in front of him, the intercom button on his telephone lit up, beeped, and he heard a familiar voice.

"Narvell. It's Bill. Can you come in here?"

Narvell stared at the phone. For the first time since he had been welcomed into the company, Bill Cooke had actually asked Narvell to his office. Narvell began to wonder what assignment Bill might give him. Then his wonder turned to panic. What if he was going to get in trouble for asking questions? What if he was in trouble for taking pictures? Had Jimbo said something to the boss? So, instead of bounding into Bill's office in anticipation of a first assignment, Narvell nervously walked down the corridor to Bill's office in the corner.

"Narvell?" Bill asked as if he had never seen the newest member of the engineering department.

"Yes, sir."

"I have an assignment for you. Some sales guy downstairs wants us to recalculate the cost of an entire product line. It's the vacuum storage vessels used by research labs to transport whatever it is they transport without fear of germs escaping or contaminating what's inside. Should probably take you about a week and a half to gather the information, plug it into the costing module, and update the records. I told Allyson, our VP of Sales, that it would be about two weeks. Get started on it right away. Here's the vessel part numbers to recalc. You'll need to drill down on the component parts," Bill said, sticking out a sheet of paper torn off of a note pad.

"Bill, I can probably have this done by Monday afternoon. If you want it done sooner, I can work this weekend," Narvell offered.

"Son, sit down. Let me explain a few things to you."

Bill very coldly began his explanation, which almost immediately set off an alarm in Narvell's head. "We run this department, come to think about it, this company, on a very rigid and exact schedule. Engineering has calculated schedules that we work by. Every other department that interacts with us knows how long it should take us to do our part. We cannot deviate from this schedule, especially with sales people, or others will begin to ask us to expedite their work every time they need something.

"Years ago, our management team decided that the only way to truly plan our work from start to finish throughout the company was to understand how long each task should take, let everyone else know how long that is, and then live by the schedule. It has worked for Engineering for ten-plus years now. In that time, I have only had one firefight that I have had to manage and that was with the chairman of the board. Afterwards, I had to explain to him and Fred what chaos his little *hot order* caused for us. Our next engineering update reflected the problem when I showed that bypassing our process pushed six other projects late. Since then, I've had no other problems living by the rules. Are you following me?"

Narvell shook his head yes and then in an almost timid tone asked, "But if we can very quickly provide the information requested, why can't we just do it and get it over with?"

"Narvell, listen to me. I just stated that as a company we live by the rules that the executive management team has set out. The rules have worked for over ten years now, and I have no desire to change them. They work. They work for me. They work for all of our directors and vice presidents. They work for our engineers and they WILL work for you.

"Our management team at the top sets these rules and they are pushed down, supported, and enforced company-wide. It is not your job to change these rules. Just do what you are told to do and you will have a long, and hopefully, successful career at M.E. Burdette. I have already logged this request into the system. You will see the power of the system when we report out to our division management team next month. Then you'll see how it all fits together when we meet with top management next quarter. Simply put, we live and breathe by our metrics. Our success as an engineering department is rooted in our metrics scorecard. You are the newbie here, so just do as I say and the world WILL treat you right. Do you understand?" Bill closed with emphasis and stood to drive his point home.

"Yes, sir. When do you want the cost calculations?" Narvell said in a very dry, flat tone.

"A week from today or the following Monday will be perfect. I can then give them to Allyson that Wednesday or Thursday, after I review them, and then we look like heroes being one day early. Get to work, son." Bill finished this statement while turning away from Narvell and picking up the telephone to make call.

***

Sitting alone at the Corner Café, Narvell stared at his sandwich as if willing it to float up to his mouth on its own. He was really staring straight past it at nothing in particular, replaying this morning's meeting with Bill in his mind. He had never eaten lunch with anyone else since he started his job at M.E. Burdette Co., and today was no exception. Just then, he heard a familiar voice shout out his name.

"Narvell! I heard you were back in town, and working for M.E.B. So why are you sitting alone and how long have you been staring at that sandwich?" said the woman as she slid into the booth across from him.

"Annie. It's good to see you, too," Narvell replied half-heartedly.

"Okay Narvie, what's wrong? I can tell something isn't right in your world."

"It's nothing I can explain over lunch. But I am glad I ran into you. Chris said you might be able to help me with something."

"You've talked to Chris? What did he say? Does he miss me?" Annie leaned in close, expecting to hear some good gossip. The reply she got was not what she expected.

"Actually, we didn't even talk about you until Chris was walking out the door."

"Wait a minute, Narvell. Are you telling me that the one and only Chris Anselmo is in town? When did this happen?" Annie said, sitting back up straight. "Why?"

Narvell could tell that not all the old feelings Annie had once had for her former boyfriend had died. "He got transferred to corporate sometime in the last few weeks. It looks like he might be back in town for good. You still interested in him, Annie?"

"Of course not, Narvell. Remember, I broke up with him. His wandering eyes, and hands, were too much. You and I talked about that after I told him it was over, remember? I am not into guys who are into more than one girl at a time. Chris is a playboy and into partying, and I want none of that. I didn't have time for it then and I sure don't now," Annie said with an added edge in her voice. "But enough about me and Chris. What's up with you? Sorry I didn't hunt you down to welcome you aboard, but I've been out of town a lot on business. And, when I'm here, I usually have no social life at all. We are trying to get new product catalogs finished and into the sales teams' hands before the end of next quarter. Guess who is just one big deadline? But come on. Tell me what's troubling you."

"Annie, it sounds like you're too busy. I'm not going to bother you with my problems. I'll work it out on my own. Don't worry about it."

"Narvell. You are my friend. I will always find time for you. Meet me after work today at Aspen's. It's a good, quiet place to talk. You can spill your heart out then. I've got to grab a sandwich and run. I have a meeting in twenty minutes. See you this evening."

And with that, Annie Gerdes, the former girlfriend of Chris Anselmo, was gone. In like a flash, out like a flash … never sitting still very long. She had a reputation for being high energy, even bouncing off the walls at times. Narvell thought about that energy she had just displayed and was reminded of the time that Chris had explained this as the source of her nickname; the Bean, as in Mexican jumping bean. Annie hadn't even given Narvell time to say yes or no to her request to meet after work. Under normal circumstances, he would have been excited at the possibility of spending time with her. But the events of the past several days had taken its toll on him. He was already worn out trying to understand the issues with his company and the losses Fred Schmidt had talked about yesterday, and now he was faced with his first real assignment as a cost analyst. He felt like he was being used by his boss, and it just wasn't sitting very well on his mind or his stomach at this moment.

Deciding that he wasn't hungry, Narvell stood up and headed for the door. Might as well start working on that assignment this afternoon.

***

All Narvell could do was stare at the computer screen. It was now 4:12 p.m. He had just spent the past three hours working on his costing assignment and had come to a rather surprising conclusion. He wasn't sure if he should say anything to Bill right now or wait until he gave him the cost analysis package a week from today. Other than not having an accurate purchased price figure for one stainless steel fastener, he knew with confidence that he had all of his cost data pulled together and entered into the prescribed form from the engineering template folder on the file server. What he wasn't sure of was how long it would take Purchasing to provide him with the information he had requested a little before 3:00 p.m.

Just then, the phone rang. He answered and was surprised to hear the voice on the other end of the line. "Narvell, this is Staci in Purchasing. I have that cost you asked about earlier. Do you want a verbal or should I e-mail it to you?"

"Wow, that was fast," replied Narvell. "Can you give the info and then send an e-mail to document it? I'll need to get it updated in the engineering cost system before I can complete my calculations."

"I'll do better than that. I've already had our purchasing assistant down here update the cost tables. I still don't know why that fastener wasn't in the system. We only buy about 140,000 of them a year. You can recalculate your part whenever you want. The price is in there for you. And, I just sent you the e-mail. Have a nice weekend, Narvell." And with that, Staci hung up the phone without even waiting for Narvell to respond.

Three minutes later, Narvell was done. But now he realized that he had another question stuck in his brain. Why was he having to pull all of his data for each part in the analysis out of the company's Enterprise Resource Planning system, or ERP, and plug it all into this spreadsheet template? As he was updating the top-level part information, he saw the buttons at the top of the screen. One simply said **Print**. And since Narvell had nothing better to do late on a Friday afternoon, he did just that. He clicked on the **Print** button and was rewarded with a printout that had detailed cost information on each part nested from top level to bottom level. The labor and overhead costs were even broken down separately at each component's level.

The other button said **Export**. Why not try this as well and see what it does? Pointing at this button on the screen, Narvell gave it a quick click and he was met with a pop-up window that said, "Export to **Text** or **Spreadsheet**?" He chose the button labeled **Spreadsheet** and a new window popped up asking for a file name. After saving the file to his desktop, Narvell opened it and found his printed report with the data labels in one column and the data in the cell to each label's right. The only difference from the printed version and the exported version was that all of the labels and data were in single columns. There was no nesting of levels. But it still gave the sum total at the bottom of the list.

Narvell found the fastener cost in the list of data contained in the printed version, added it into his file that he had created with the required template, and then clicked on one of the finished goods part numbers on the tabs at the bottom of his screen. He looked at the total for this item and then compared it against the number on the printed report. His total using the engineering form was 11.7% lower than what had been printed directly out of the ERP. Narvell checked each of the parts in his report and found that the cost calculated matched none of what was showing in ERP. This was the source of his dilemma. Why transfer all this data from ERP to a spreadsheet if the numbers didn't match? But which number was correct? It was obvious to Narvell that something was missing from his spreadsheet. But what?

After only ninety seconds of searching, he found his answer. The calculation of overhead dollars being reported for purchased parts in his spreadsheet was being subtracted from the cost of the part instead of being added to the total cost. It was a simple mathematical error. Narvell corrected the formula on each tab of the spreadsheet and compared totals once more. Everything matched. He saved his file and closed it. He would review it all one more time first thing Monday before discussing it with Bill.

Feeling satisfied with his success of the afternoon, Narvell, in a burst of renewed energy, decided to focus on the company's financial problem again. It was then that he remembered what he had found in the metrics folder earlier in the day. He immediately made his way through the maze of folders and subfolders back to the one labeled: Outside Sales—Northeast Region. Opening the metrics file once again, Narvell read through what was in front of him on the screen. How had he missed this folder and file before?

OUTSIDE SALES – NORTHEAST REGION

UOM	BASELINE	PREVIOUS	% CHANGE	CURRENT	%CHANGE
Sales Dollars (Qtr)	374,001	479,115	28.1↑	636,899	32.9%↑
Gross Margin	27.2%	34.4%	26.5%↑	40.9%	18.9%↑
Cost of Sales (%)	27.3%	21.3%	22.0%↓	16.0%	24.9%↓

Narvell read the data on the screen several times and then leaned back in his chair. Here was yet one more example of an area in the company where it appeared as though everything was going as well as could be expected. Sales were up. Margins were up. And even the costs of closing the sales, reported as a percentage of sales, were going down. At least that was the way Narvell interpreted what was on the screen. If every part of the company was doing this well, why are we losing money? Maybe this will provide a clue to the answer of Chris' question from last night, thought Narvell as he printed out a copy of the metrics and tucked them into his shirt pocket. "I'll show these to Annie and ask her what she knows about this sales team," Narvell said quietly to himself as he logged off his computer and headed for the door.

***

After finishing off his second beer and more than his share of the chips and salsa sitting on the table in front of them, Narvell was beginning to loosen up a bit. Still he wasn't comfortable enough to start the conversation with Annie about what was bothering him. It just didn't seem quite right that the new kid on the block would be worried about the financial affairs of the company and how the director of engineering conducted business, while Annie, who had been employed by the company since the week after she graduated from college over a year earlier, was sitting apparently without a worry in the world.

Several times since Narvell had arrived at Aspen's Lounge as requested by Annie earlier in the day, she had practically jumped from her seat to greet someone else coming through the restaurant. She would engage them in animated conversation, and then promise to meet up with them at some time in the future. Then she would come back to the table and pick up the conversation right where they had left off.

But suddenly Annie's face grew dead serious. She leaned across the table and said in a calm yet firm tone, "Okay Narvell, spit it out. What is wrong?

You looked like you were totally lost today at lunch, and when you came in here you seemed completely distracted. Tell me right now."

"You sure you have time for this?"

"Yes. You shouldn't even have to ask. Go."

"All right. It has to do with work," Narvell began.

"And …," Annie trailed off as she looked Narvell in the eyes.

"I went to my first goals and objectives meeting this week. You know that quarterly update meeting that Mr. Schmidt does with management and the engineers." But before Narvell could get any further, Annie began to laugh. "Fine. Be that way. Just forget it, Annie. I knew I shouldn't have said anything." Narvell started to stand up to leave.

"Sit down, Narvell. I'm not laughing at you. I'm laughing about that stupid meeting. It's referred to in my office as the *CYA* meeting … nothin' but a bunch of shirts proving how good they are. So what's the problem?"

"We're losing money as a company and no one seems to care. Mr. Schmidt got mad and was obviously frustrated, yet no one seemed to have any answers for him. I talked to one of the engineers afterwards, and Jimbo's response made it sound like everything would be fine by next month. How the heck does that work?" Narvell was suddenly feeling very passionate about the topic at hand, and not sure whether it was the alcohol giving him courage or if he finally had had enough. He could tell that now was his opportunity to see if anyone inside M.E. Burdette Co. felt like he did. "It just amazes me that there was this entire room full of people, and not one person spoke up about what the root cause of the problem might have been."

"So what exactly did Schmidt say about the financial stability of the company, Narvell?" Annie interrupted as she drew in closer at the table, so Narvell would not have to speak in a loud voice over the background music and other conversations in the room.

"He simply stated that he had no idea about why we're losing money if everyone was meeting their goals. When no one spoke up, he appeared to get mad and said he wanted Bill, Dane, and Allyson to figure it out. So now I guess Engineering, Manufacturing, and Sales will put together some report showing what is happening. Mr. Schmidt will be happy, the board will be happy, and none of the rest of us will have a clue what is really happening."

"Narvell, why do you care? Shouldn't you be focusing on cost analysis and getting some good experience for the future?"

"Are you telling me, Annie, that no one is concerned?"

"I'm sure that upper level management is concerned. After all, their bonuses all depend on the financial success of the company. But why are you so worked up about it?" Annie asked in a very inquisitive tone.

"I guess it's because I'm a *numbers* guy. This is not exactly what I thought I'd be doing when I got out of school, but it's a start. That little alarm in my head went off the other day when no one spoke up. And then again, when Bill Cooke *explained* to me exactly how he wanted me to do my job, on his schedule to make him look good. There was no interest in efficiency. He just wants his numbers. Live or die by his rules is how I took it. Add that to all the comments Jimbo has made to me, and, of course, I suspect something isn't quite right. Don't you ever get those feelings?"

"Narvell, I work in Marketing. I feel very lucky to be working for the man I work for. I have never seen anyone in a management position in Marketing as ethical and moral as George. He's not a VP, but he should be. He constantly reminds us that our job is to ethically portray our products to the customer. He won't even let you cross over into a gray area when you write text expounding on the positive aspects of the product. He reminds us that honesty was what made this company what it is today, and that we must remember this as we all move up in the organization. It's as if he expects each of his staff to get promoted out from under him. Almost as if that's his goal. So, do I get suspicious of what goes on in Marketing? No. Do I ever wonder about what goes on in other parts of the company? Yes, I do on occasion. Not that I spend a lot of time with other departments. But, every once in a while I second-guess something I hear out of one of the Sales divisions or Engineering. So, now that I know the basis of your worries, what now?"

"Well, I'm not sure. When I talked to Chris about this last night, he ended the conversation by asking me about a tape measure. He told me to go find mine. But I don't even know what he's talking about," Narvell said as his emotional sail began to deflate.

This drew a big laugh from Annie. "I know what he's talking about, sort of. I got to hear his father and grandfather talking about different people's tape measures when I was dating Chris and we'd go to his parents' house for dinner. I really never got a full explanation about it. But I know that it has something to do with a manager's measurements within their department. So, what did Chris tell you?"

"He just asked me what my tape measure was and then told me to go get as much info as I could about the situation. I have an incredible amount of data that I collected from the metrics board by the break room, but Chris said he didn't think the answer to his question was in that mountain of data. We're supposed to get together next Friday, I think, to talk about it. Want to come along?" Narvell said without really thinking that it might be awkward for Annie or Chris to put them together socially again.

"I'm supposed to be in Chicago at the end of the week. Not sure when I'll get home. I'll call you. Gotta run. I told Delaney (you remember her from college, don't you?) that I'd meet her later for dinner. Totally forgot about it when I told you to meet me this evening. Did I help any?" Annie asked as she started to stand up.

"Maybe. I've got to think about all this."

"Okay. Here's my cell number. Call me any time," Annie said as she handed Narvell her business card. "See you later, Narv." And with that, Annie rushed across the bar area of the restaurant and out the door.

It suddenly occurred to Narvell that he had not asked her about the Northeast Region Sales Metrics he had in his pocket.

***

Back home in his bedroom, Narvell fired up his computer and immediately logged into his blog. After the day he had had and meeting with Annie, he thought he actually had something more to chew on in regards to his journey for understanding.

More Questions...

Posted on **September 9, 2011**
Reply

Got my first cost analysis assignment today. Thought I'd be more excited about it. But when your boss tells you to take a week to do a job that only took a couple of hours, you kind of lose that excitement. It feels as if Bill is playing games with the rest of company. Stretching out deadlines to make sure that Engineering is never late. And then the department looks great when he delivers one day early.

Question: Maybe I need to see what the average delivery time to the customer is? I think I saw a metric on the Big Board about that. I need to look on Monday. Can't quite make it out on the photos I took with my phone.

Question: Why are we not using the ERP system for costing? I forgot to mention that to Annie.

Question: Remember to ask Annie about the Northeast Sales Region! Why do they only have three metrics in their file? Are there more on the Big Board? Need to look on Monday.

Annie mentioned that her boss preached ethical behavior and that this was a guiding principle of the company. Bill also preached about living by the company rules. Is there any correlation in these two statements?
AM I ANY CLOSER?

Posted in Blogs from the book | Leave a reply

Chapter 4

What Are We Doing *Wrong*?

September 12

Monday morning came and went with Narvell doing little more than reviewing the work he had completed Friday afternoon. He had sat in on a project meeting run by Jimbo. Since he had attended every meeting Jimbo had held on this project to date, he felt like it was the right thing to do. He didn't want the engineers on the team to think that he wasn't interested in their project anymore.

After the meeting, he stopped by Bill's office to discuss the formula error he had found in the template. The lights were out and based upon the amount of papers sitting in Bill's chair, it appeared as though he had not been in the office this morning. So, Narvell went back to his cubicle and compared his cost analysis report line by line against the report printed out of the ERP system. When he was done, Narvell was completely satisfied that he had all of his cost figures correct. Just as he saved his file and closed it, Jimbo appeared looking over the side of his cubicle.

"Hey Narvell, what do you think? Does it look like I'll be able to wrap up my project by the final milestone date on the Gantt chart?"

"Why are you asking me? I'm just a cost analyst and an observer on your project. Not that I don't appreciate you letting me sit in, but what can I possibly add to the conversation?"

"You're an outsider. There's great value in that. I love to hear what other people have to say about the way I run my projects. That's how I get better at what I do. So …"

"Well, yeah, I suppose you'll beat your deadline assuming you can get the material quotes back from Purchasing on time and that you can solve that seal problem on the lid. But, I don't really see the quotes as an issue. Not after the quick response I got on my fastener quote last Friday. Since I'm not an engineer, I doubt I can give you a good answer on the seal problem. Jimbo, have you got a minute to look at something?" Narvell decided midstream in this conversation to show Jimbo the error he had found on Friday.

"Sure. What's up?" Jimbo asked as he came into the cubicle and sat down in the side chair. Narvell showed him the template located on the file server, and then showed him the formula that he found that contained the error. Finally, he showed him the corrected formula in his cost analysis file he had completed Friday afternoon.

"What do you think? Turn about is fair play, isn't it? Do you think I should just change the formula in the template and move on, or should I show it to Bill? It looks like the last time the template was updated was about four years ago. I wonder how many parts we've run a cost analysis on, during that time, that went out wrong."

"If I were you, I'd ask Bill about the formula, and then if he tells you something different than is in the template, show it to him. If he explains it the way it's written, I'd just move on. Bill is the one that developed that template and from everything I've ever seen, he's pretty proud of it," Jimbo said in a quiet tone; almost as though he didn't want anyone in the area to overhear him.

"But it's wrong. I know it is. We need to get it right. Isn't that why I was hired?"

"No, Narvell you were hired to do costing for the engineering team. Bill hired you with certain expectations and if you know what is good for you, you'll live up to those expectations. Besides, there's not much you can do about it right now. Bill's out of town this week. The first chance you'll have to speak with him is next Monday. Just sit on all this until Friday afternoon and then e-mail your report to Bill. Let him review it and if you really want to discuss the formula with him, do it after that. And be careful how you present the issue. That is my friendly piece of advice for the day." And with that, Jimbo stood up and headed for his own cubicle.

Since there was not a lot more Narvell could do about his assignment or the formula error, he decided he might as well spend the rest of the week answering the questions he'd asked himself in his blog Friday night. He pulled the blog page up on his screen and then spent the rest of the week splitting his time between Jimbo's project meetings and his review of the metrics posted on the Big Board, as he was now calling it, outside the break room. The focus of his many trips down to The Big Board was centered on Engineering and Sales. The search was on. The question was … would he find anything?

***

Friday evening came and Narvell actually found himself somewhat excited about having dinner with Chris and discussing the whole financial picture thing. And, he was very curious at this point to learn more about Chris' tape measure questions from the week before. For some reason, though, he just wished that Annie would have been able to come. She had called last night to say that she was staying in Chicago with friends for the weekend since they hadn't gotten through with their customer surveys during the week. She would be home late Monday night, but said she wanted a blow-by-blow description of Narvell and Chris' conversation on the topic at hand.

While Narvell and Chris stood over the barbecue grill in Narvell's backyard, they made small talk about a few old friends bringing each other up to date on where they were and/or what they were doing. About the time the hamburgers were cooked to both their satisfactions, Chris brought up Narvell's quest.

"Well, what new information did you find in the past week, my friend?" Chris asked as he flipped the last burger off onto a plate Narvell was holding.

"I'm not sure. I spent a good deal of time reviewing the Big Board. I focused most of my time looking at the engineering and sales metrics. But to be quite honest, I may be more confused about the numbers now than I was before."

"Why so?"

"I must have reviewed the engineering numbers eight or ten times this week and they seem perfect. Actually, almost too perfect. But I can't find a hole in them. The one thing I did find that makes me feel better is the turn-around time metric for engineering requests. The metric itself is not shown as elapsed time, but as the difference between due date and delivery date," Narvell explained as he opened the back door for Chris to go inside.

"And why does this make you feel better?" asked Chris.

Narvell then explained the verbal exchange with Bill over his cost analysis assignment. "That little alarm went off in my head when Bill laid down the law with me," Narvell concluded.

"And so, the million dollar question then is how is engineering doing against this metric?" pushed Chris as he starting making his burger at Narvell's kitchen cabinet. Just then, Bobby came lumbering into the kitchen.

"Something smells good. You guys make enough for me?" asked Bobby as he opened the refrigerator and grabbed a beer.

"Absolutely," Chris chimed in without hesitation even though Narvell was shaking his head no. "Grab a plate, Bobby."

Sitting down at the table on the back deck after all three men had filled their plates, Chris started up the conversation once more. "Back up to the metric issue again. How is Engineering doing against the metric?"

"We are beating our stated due dates by 0.82 days on average. There is a second measurement that shows the range. Minimally, we go from a –1.0 to a +1.25."

Bobby looked up from his plate and cut off any chance of Chris or Narvell continuing the conversation. "What the hell are you guys talking about? You're not still on that missing money topic from last week are you? I told you guys then that your boss, Narvell, is stealing from the company. Can't we change the subject?"

Before Narvell could tell Bobby to shut up, Chris answered in a very firm and to-the-point voice, "Bobby, this subject is the reason I'm here tonight. If you don't like the topic, you can always eat and run. No one is keeping you here."

"Okay then," Bobby answered back. "If I'm staying, then please explain what that –1.0 to +1.25 thing means. I think I came in on the middle of it."

"Our Engineering Department measures itself on how well they respond to internal customer requests. When the request is turned in, they assign a due date based upon the type of request. Then they track how they respond against that due date. The range is from being one day later to being one and a quarter days early. The reported average or mean is 0.82 days early. So now you are caught up. May I continue?" Narvell responded.

Without waiting for a reply, Narvell went on. "If I had been allowed to do my job and respond to the cost request I got last week, the range on the early side would have been about 9.75 days. I just wonder how many times other department employees have sat on their work waiting on the due date?"

"Narvell, I think you are onto something here. Let's go back to our conversation from the other day. Do you want to talk to me about your tape measure yet?" Chris said with a curious smile on his face.

"No. I want you to explain it to me."

"That's not the way it works. Granddad says that everyone has to understand the power of their tape measure before they can use it. You have to 'see it' and be able to 'read it' with confidence before it becomes real." Chris used his hands to make quote signs on each side of the words *see it* and *read it* to add the emphasis he wanted to make for Narvell on this point.

"So since you don't appear ready to talk about your tape measure yet, let's move on. What else you got?" Chris went on.

"While it looks like I see what Bill is doing with his numbers, I'm totally baffled by some of the sales numbers. There must be twice as many metrics on the Big Board for the sales teams as there are for Engineering. Yet, the Northeast Region Sales team only has three metrics, period. And still, if you look at team growth in sales, they lead the company. How can you do that only measuring three things?"

Chris' smile got bigger at hearing Narvell's question. "Bingo! I think we may have a winner. Why do you need more than three measurements to know how you are doing?"

"Well, look at all the variables involved in running a sales team. You have individual results. You have major customers and the occasional customer. How do you track all of this with only three numbers? How do you all do it at Housholder?"

"Are you asking me for the answer or for insight here, Narv?"

"Yes. I'll take anything you can give me. I really want to know what's going on, and whether or not I'll even have a job in a year."

"I tell you what. If you will do an exercise that I know all of our managers go through, I'll let you in on what I know about the tape measure. But, since neither of us have a lot of real-world experience, we'll work through it together. You can feed information into the equation on what happens at Burdette and I'll add the facts as I know them for Housholder."

Chris got up from his seat on the deck and looked not at Narvell, but at Bobby. "Bob, my man, this is your last chance to make any smart ass remarks you may have about the situation. So, you better go for it now. From this point on, we are going to be deadly serious about the situation. Well …?"

Not letting the opportunity pass him by, Bobby took a large swig of beer, belched, and then said, "I still say Narvell's boss is stealing from the company. I bet he made off with thousands of dollars. And, I don't think you two novices have a bat's chance in hell of figuring it out. He's too smart and has been getting away with it for too long to allow you to catch him. I know I don't really know a thing about your company, Narvell, but this always drunk, slightly crazy, and forever if I can manage it, perpetual student knows a thing or two about how to outfox a corrupt organization. I have spent a lifetime watching my father outfox people legally in the financial markets. Okay, I'm done. See you boys later." And with that, Bobby Evans was off the deck and headed for the back gate to destinations unknown; not that Narvell or Chris really cared.

"Narvell, here is how this will work. I'll explain the tape measure to you and in return we will compare the old traditional way to the new and creative way. You will represent the old traditional and I will be the new creative."

"What the heck are you talking about now?" Narvell interrupted.

"Burdette is a very old school, traditional manufacturing company, right?" Chris asked, and Narvell nodded in agreement. "And even though Housholder Sprockets is not a new company, we have always thought outside the box … or so my father and granddad say. So you will represent your company, I will represent mine. Together we will conduct the exercise granddad requires of all of our managers as part of the on-boarding process. If you can't do the exercise, you get let go; immediately. We do this, and in return, I explain the tape measure. Agreed?"

"Sure," responded Narvell. "I'll play your silly game. If it gets me where I want to end up, I'll try anything. So how do we do it?"

"I'll explain the tape measure and then you can do your part over the weekend. I want you to list the things that make M.E. Burdette Co. who it is. List the guiding principles, how you measure success, how you prepare for the future. Detail the most important metrics you use as a company; your Key Performance Indicators (KPIs). I think the easiest way to accomplish all this is to create a list on your blog. We can use a two-column format and after you are done, I'll add the list of how Housholder does it. After all that, we can talk about the tape measure and how all this fits together. What do you think?"

"Chris, you know I have never shown my blog to anyone. I have it password protected because I don't want anyone, especially you, looking at my most private thoughts. This is how I get things off my chest. How I decompress at times. There is no way I'm doing that."

"Great. Then no explanation on the tape measure," Chris responded and just stared at Narvell.

After what seemed like an eternity to both men, Narvell finally spoke. "It's obvious that you are not going to bend on this, huh? How about if I copy my blog entries that pertain to this into a new blog, and we keep it password protected. Just you and me? Does that work?"

"You the man, Narv! Okay, set it up tonight and e-mail me the URL and password. I promise not to look until you are done. Send me an e-mail, and then I'll do my part. Ready to hear the tale of the tape measure?"

Chapter 5

The Tape Measure

Narvell had gotten each of them another beer and had settled back into his chair out on the deck. As the sun was setting, it had begun to cool off on this early autumn evening. Narvell could not have cared less at this point. He was ready for Chris' explanation of his tape measure question from the week before.

Chris began with a simple disclaimer. "If I don't get this completely correct, please don't shoot me. I'm going to explain it to you as I remember it from hearing dad and granddad tell the story to others they knew when trying to explain our company's success. And please don't interrupt me. Let me get all the way through it before you start asking questions. That's what granddad says he always tells our managers when he discusses it with them for the first time.

"The tape measure is the simplest of tools and yet can handle incredibly complex tasks. Think of the carpenter and how he uses his tape measure. One day he is building a house. While he's framing the house, his tape measure is most likely being used to measure his lumber in 1/8" increments as he saws the boards to build the frame. That's close enough for framing purposes. Right? Don't answer me. It's a rhetorical question. There's always the perfectionist, and when he's framing his house he probably uses his tape measure to measure lumber to within 1/16", or for the obsessive-compulsive disorder (OCD) carpenter that has to be absolutely perfect, he measures the boards to within 1/32".

"Then he has to cut each board, right? What's the blade thickness on the saw? 1/8" generally speaking. How good are the carpenter's eyes? Good enough to lay those boards up on the saw and cut them with precision to

1/32 of an inch? Probably not. That's why most carpenters go for the 1/8"
accuracy. It's close enough. Oh, and don't forget about the uneven areas
on your stem wall. Get the cuts to within 1/8" and the world is good. That
carpenter can frame a pretty good house using the tape measure this way.
Then the carpenter gets around to trimming out the house; putting up fascia
boards, you know, installing trim pieces on the outside of the house. This
same carpenter may then use that same tape measure and spend a bit more
time being more accurate. Now he's measuring to within a 1/16 of an inch.
He takes more time setting his boards on the saw to get the cut closer. He
wants the finished product to match the effort he has just put into it.

"Then that same carpenter may build the cabinets and install trim inside
the house. Does he use the 1/32" marks on his tape measure? Maybe.
Depends on how good his eyes are, how accurate his marks are, and how
straight and new the blade on his saw is. But once again … he is looking for
perfection based upon his expectations. He wants his customer to approve.

"And how does customer approval happen? Or for that matter, how do
you get past the government code inspections? When an inspector comes
in and he is measuring clearance from wiring to plumbing, or distance
between wall studs, does the inspector use that 1/8" unit of measure? Of
course not. He slaps that tape measure up against what he is measuring
and looks at the inches unit of measure. The homeowner, wanting to make
sure the ceilings are going to be the right height, may grab that carpenter's
tape measure and quickly throw it up against a wall from floor to ceiling.
Chances are he is looking at the feet unit of measure.

"The point of this story is that the tape measure can be used one way by
one person and another way by the next. How many of us have ever used
the centimeter side of a tape measure? Not many in the United States, I bet.
But it is there on some tape measures for those people that want or need to
use it.

"The trick is to always know what your tape measure is. Not where it is, but
what it is. Granddad says if you know the unit of measure that equals success in
business, you know your tape measure. It's all about knowing and understanding, in the simplest of terms, what success means for your company.

"At Housholder Sprockets, Inc. our CEO, my grandfather, has a tape measure. What he measures with it is the overall success of the company. Most
people would call that our Key Performance Indicators or KPIs. That is what
granddad is interested in. That is his tape measure. And as granddad and my
father hire each executive and manager into the company, they ask the new
hires, 'What is your tape measure?' They ask them to reach back into their

past experiences and look at the way they measured success. They expect each person to list all the things that they measured to show how successful they were. Then they start questioning each item on the list. Granddad's goal is to pare that list down to create that person's tape measure.

"He does all of this in a learning environment. He lets each person go through the exercise of understanding the good, the bad, and the ugly; his words not mine, of how businesses measure success. As they work through the list, participants are often asked to go back into the areas they manage and focus on a single item. Then they discuss that item in detail at a later date to see how effective it truly is in measuring success. Once the list has been pared down sufficiently, they get asked the big question. How does each of the remaining items explain the success of their area to the employees that work for that manager, and how do the items relate to the tape measure of the person above them? After all, think back to the carpenter. There is a relationship between the way the carpenter uses that tape measure, the way the inspector uses it, and the way the homeowner uses it. Each one is after the same thing, and there is a relationship that must be maintained.

"As a result of this practice, our management team is much more focused on success than many of our competitors. And, it has worked for many years. Granddad only asks four things of our management team:

1. Find the tape measure for your area of responsibility.
2. You must have extremely high personal ethics, which shall always guide your way.
3. Treat all of your employees with the highest respect.
4. Understand that if any employee of the company fails at one of these three guiding principles, he or she will not be an employee at the end of the day.

"As a company, we are committed to these principles. I told you the story of my father having to fire a really good friend. There are no exceptions. If you can't, or won't, find your tape measure you will not be a part of our team. If you stumble on any ethical issue, do not expect to be here tomorrow. And if you do not respect your employees, you will not be a good fit for the company in the long run. Too many companies allow managers to develop a chasm between themselves and the workers. It hurts the employees, the manager, and the company. So why do it?

"So, Narvell, what is your tape measure?" Chris concluded, looking at a completely speechless Narvell.

Finally, Narvell sat up in his chair, took a drink of his beer, and opened his mouth. The problem was no words came out. He had so many things running through his mind at that moment that he didn't know where to start. After numerous false starts, Narvell managed to blurt out, "You have got to be kidding me! Right?"

Chris looked Narvell square in the eyes and responded, "Nope. Not one bit. And I assume you are saying that about the tape measure, not the guiding principles."

"Yeah. I think the principles are great other than number one. How in the world do you expect me to believe that tale?"

Chris' response seemed almost planned. "You've heard of the KISS principle, right? *Keep It Simple Stupid.* That is how granddad got here. He built houses when he was young. He worked for a guy who used to say 'KISS' every time granddad asked how the guy could work so fast and always get his measurements and cuts right. The lesson stuck. When granddad went into business for himself, he remembered that one single lesson above all else, and so he always told his employees to keep it simple. One day when he explained why he leaned so heavily on this idea to an employee, the guy responded, 'So you want me to measure success with a tape measure.' They laughed about it then, but from that point on granddad had a mission, and a story, to get every one of his managers to understand what he meant about measuring success. So, I ask you a question, Narvell. How does Burdette measure success?"

Narvell thought through all of the metrics on the Big Board at Burdette. He thought about Jimbo's explanation about how Bill, Dane, and Allyson would come up with an answer for Mr. Schmidt and the board. He thought about Bill's rules for succeeding in Engineering and how he needed to live within those established guidelines. Then he started seeing all the metrics on the Big Board again. As he sat quietly contemplating the situation, Chris responded by sitting quietly, not moving, or distracting him in any way. After what must have been a full five minutes, Narvell finally looked at Chris and just said, "Oh."

Chapter 6

Finding Your Tape Measure

After sitting in silence for what seemed like an eternity, Chris finally stood up and faced Narvell. "Look Narv, I didn't mean to make it worse. But I think maybe I did. It's obvious that you have a lot to think about. After you've digested this some, please do what I suggested. Not just for you, but for me as well. I may be a bit selfish here, but if you can go through the exercise and list everything that you think makes Burdette who it is …. You know … how does Burdette measure success? How does Burdette run the business? If you can do that, I'll complete the second half of the work and list what Housholder's is. I want to do this for me as much as for you. Why? Because, as you used to say to me in college, 'Here comes the jerk in Chris … always thinking about himself and no one else.' Well you weren't entirely wrong. But someday I'll be the guy running Housholder. I want to be the best I can be. For a long time, I didn't think I wanted to do this. But, since I've gotten to know so many people in our company over the past year, I realize that it is up to us, my granddad, my father, and even me, to make sure that all these really good people have jobs. I want to do it because it will give me a leg up when granddad goes through this same exercise with me. I'll have to use life experience, not Housholder experience since I haven't worked anywhere else. Please Narvell, if not for you, then for me."

Narvell stood up, walked over to Chris and gave him a pat on the back. "You bet I'll go through with it. You just gave me the first decent bit of advice I've heard since I started at Burdette. I want to know if this is really a place where I want to work. I'll set up the new blog tonight and e-mail you the password. You can read through everything I've written to date. But, I'm warning you, so far it's not much. It may take me a few days or so to complete my part, though. I'm going to have to pick Annie's brain for some of this information. For that matter, I may have to pick a lot of people's brains for information. I'll talk to you later. Thanks. You've been a big help." And with that, Chris headed across the overgrown backyard desperately in need of a mowing and then through the back gate as Narvell went inside to start on his assignment from Chris.

***

The rest of the weekend was rather uneventful for Narvell and his assignment. He had hoped to spend time with Annie picking her brain about their company and how it operated and measured success. But she had decided to stay in Chicago, and they had played telephone tag off and on all day Saturday and Sunday morning. Narvell knew that she would be tied up most of Monday morning finishing up her work in Chicago and figured that it would be best just to wait for her to get home Monday night to discuss the topic, so, he gave up trying to reach her early Sunday afternoon.

When Narvell walked into the office Monday morning, he was surprised at the unusual amount of noise and activity already taking place in Engineering. When he sat down in his cubicle and turned on his computer, he found out why. Awaiting him in his e-mail inbox was a very short, yet direct, e-mail from Bill Cooke addressed to all engineering staff. The message was short and to the point. All staff members were to meet in the Engineering conference room at 8:30 a.m. with all metrics and project updates in hand. But it was the final line that caught Narvell's attention: "YOUR JOB IS ON THE LINE!" That certainly explained the chaos in the department.

As Narvell sat and stared at the screen, he began to wonder what he could add to this conversation. He had been on the job now for a month, had sat through a confusing meeting that was intended to enlighten management, but had done nothing more than confuse Narvell, and now his job was being threatened. He did breathe a bit easier when he realized that this was an e-mail to the entire department. But the uneasy feeling in his stomach didn't go away.

Since Narvell wasn't responsible for reporting out any metrics and the only project he had was the costing update he had completed last week, he decided he had better print out his information and take it with him to the meeting. Then he sat and thought about what this impromptu meeting might be about. Has something else happened? Did Bill, Dane, and Allyson not give satisfactory answers to the board? Why was Bill gone most of last week? What if my job really does get eliminated? And with that last question, another lighter and much more meaningful thought popped into Narvell's head. So what if you lose your job. It's already stressing you out. The positive is that you live with a rich, perpetual student who has had several roommates live rent free for months in the past. Maybe this won't be such a bad thing if I get canned. And with that, Narvell gathered his file and headed down the hall for the conference room.

Walking in, Narvell found a seat next to Jimbo against the back wall of the room. The 12 chairs at the table were already filled by engineers with stacks of files in front of them. Around the wall on both sides and across the back wall where Narvell and Jimbo were seated, chairs were quickly filling up with the other 14 or 15 employees who were in the office that day. And then promptly at 8:30, in walked Bill with Mr. Schmidt.

Not waiting for everyone to stop their side conversations and settle in, Mr. Schmidt spoke with a serious tone in his voice and without a hint of a smile on his face. No pleasantries, he simply started talking as if he had been on hold from the past week's meeting. "We must understand why we are losing money when other manufacturers in our industry and in our community are turning healthy profits. Right here in town, Housholder reported record quarterly profits. The board wants to know why and how that can be happening … if we are falling off a financial cliff. I met Thursday with Bill and our executive team and discussed the issues. What I was able to glean from the day was that Engineering is rock solid on metrics and that almost no project from this department misses any deadline. So I asked Bill to gather you all together today so that we can see how you all do it and can apply that to the rest of the company."

Fred Schmidt then turned to Bill as if he was waiting on him to take over the meeting. Bill seemed to be caught by surprise, and after an awkward pause, managed to regain his composure enough to ask the engineer closest to him to go over the metrics for which he was responsible. In turn, each engineer at the table explained the metrics they tracked, or where they were progress-wise on their current project. By the time this update exercise got around to the back wall of the room, both Narvell and Jimbo were fighting to keep their eyes open. Finally, the engineer to Narvell's left finished explaining the current project she was responsible for and why she thought her team was able to hit their milestones.

Just as Narvell pulled the papers out of his file to begin explaining what he was working on, Jimbo leaned forward and began to speak. "Mr. Schmidt, as you know I am responsible for customized change projects for existing customers." Narvell sat back in his chair not knowing whether to be

offended or thankful that he had not been allowed to speak. Jimbo continued on for a full ten minutes, explaining what he and his team had been
working on, giving praise to his team members throughout the company
for being so available and dedicated to getting these projects completed
on time. When he was done, Jimbo leaned back and, without looking at
Narvell, patted him on the leg.

The final three engineers along the back wall finished explaining the
projects they were working on and all three gave rather lengthy explanations about why they were staying on task and hitting their milestones
throughout the process. As Narvell sat and listened to these final three, a
thought came to him. Each and every person in the room had given their
input as to why they were all on time. And yet, not one single person in the
room had bothered to mention that many of these projects had such long
lead times on their project plans that, in Narvell's opinion, there was no way
they could miss the milestones. Narvell started to say something about this,
but then thought better of it. What if I'm missing something here? Perhaps I
still don't know enough to speak up. And with that, Narvell leaned back in
his chair and waited to see what was going to happen next.

"Very impressive, Bill. You've got a hell of a team here. I want you all to
get together and come up with a plan that explains your methodology and
how you stay on track. Be prepared to explain it to me and the exec team
Thursday morning," said Fred Schmidt as he headed for the door. Everyone
in the room, including Bill, just sat there as if some unseen force was holding them in their seats. A good twenty seconds after the door closed, Bill
finally spoke up. "Okay you all. You heard the man. I want everyone to
type your ideas on why we are successful and e-mail them to Paula this
afternoon. She can then spend tomorrow and Wednesday putting something
together that we can present to Fred on Thursday." And with that, Bill got
up and walked out.

Slowly everyone got up and headed back for their offices or cubicles. It
was unusually quiet as the engineering staff made their way to their destinations. Narvell did not, however, head for his little corner of the world.
Instead, he followed Jimbo to his office. Not waiting for Jimbo to put down
his files or even acknowledge his presence, Narvell started in. "What was
that all about back there? Why didn't you let me say anything? I am perfectly
capable of reporting what I am working on."

"Whoa, junior. Hang on a second," Jimbo responded, sitting down and
holding up both hands as if to keep Narvell from attacking him. "I simply
tried to speed that mess up and get us out of there. Did you really have

anything constructive to add? Your questions over the past week or two suggest that you're pretty darn smart, Narvell. Maybe too smart for your own good! Unless you had a silver bullet for Bill and Fred in there, I doubt there was anything you could have said that would have helped. I merely tried to get us to an end point, and I think skipping over you saved us all a couple of minutes."

"You're right, Jimbo. I apologize. I just don't get it," responded Narvell, sitting down in the chair across from Jimbo's desk. "Every single person in that room had a variety of reasons for why they are successful, but no one mentioned what I think is obvious. Bill *told me* when my costing assignment was going to be due. What I thought I could do in a couple of days at the most, he said would take me a good week and then some. Several of the projects of yours that I've sat in on have ridiculously long deadlines; even some of your team members have commented on how much time you have. Yet, no one mentioned that fact. What gives?"

Jimbo leaned forward and in a very low and steady voice replied, "Don't go there, Narvell. Bill will hand you your head on a platter. The entire engineering team has seen him end people's careers over small things, and this is not a small thing you are talking about. Each and every project gets reviewed by Bill when the project charter is completed. He has made his reputation on hitting deadlines dead on. If he thinks there isn't enough wiggle room, he changes the dates before the team starts. Please, Narvell. I like you, kid. Don't cross this line with him."

"Okay, okay. I get it. I'll keep my mouth shut. But, can I come and talk to you about this stuff when I get frustrated or confused?" Narvell offered as he stood up.

"Yes. Definitely. Any time you want."

"Thank you, Jimbo." And with that Narvell left Jimbo's office and went back to his cubicle.

Just as Narvell was sitting down his phone rang. "This is Narvell."

"Narvell. Where have you been? I've been calling all morning," Annie said through the phone.

"We just had another one of those sessions with Mr. Schmidt. Everyone on staff had to give another update and explain why they are successful. Everyone but me, that is. Jimbo cut me off before I could say a word, and nobody circled back and asked me to speak. So, once again I sit like a bump on a log and just ask questions to myself. When are you coming home? I need to talk to you and the sooner the better," Narvell responded with a hint of desperation in his voice.

"Narvell, calm down. What's going on?"

"I'm not sure. But I don't think I like it. We got a threatening e-mail from Bill this morning and then we met with him and Schmidt. Everyone talked about how great we are, but no one said a word about the real reason we make all our deadlines."

"Okay. Calm down. I'm coming in on the 5:30 flight this afternoon. I need a ride home, so pick me up at the airport, and we can go get dinner and talk. I'll call you when my plane is on the ground and tell you where to pick me up. Gotta run. I have one more meeting before I get out of here. See you this evening. Bye." And with that, Annie was gone.

Narvell sat and thought about the whole situation for nearly an hour and then decided about the only thing he could do was to work on his assignment from Chris. He logged on to his computer, opened his web browser, and navigated his way to his blog. Once he had entered his password and was staring at the new blog he had set up, he started to write what he knew, or more appropriately, what he thought he knew.

He was lost in his thoughts and writing when, all of a sudden, he realized that Jimbo was staring at him over the cubicle wall. "Young Mr. Mann, would you like to grab a bite for lunch with a crusty old engineer who has been kinda hard on you the last few days?"

"Absolutely, Jimbo. Let me save this and I'll be ready to go." Narvell said as he saved his work and closed his web browser. "Where are we going?"

"Well, since I have a 1:30 meeting with Bill on the hot topic of the day, we better make it a quick one over at the Corner Café. You mind?"

"Not at all. One of my favorite lunch hangouts … has been since my freshman year in college. We'd come over here on days when we couldn't figure out what the cafeteria food on campus was," Narvell responded with a laugh.

"Good to see you loosening up a bit, Narvell."

***

After placing their order, Narvell and Jimbo made small talk discussing college football and how unseasonably warm it was. Then Jimbo broke the ice. "So what were you writing when I came to get you for lunch? You were way too focused on your keyboard. You aren't still trying to solve the company's problems all by yourself, are you?"

"Not at all. I'm trying to understand all of this, and one way is for me to blog about what I know … which, by the way, isn't very much, apparently. I kept trying to write down everything I've learned since that first meeting of Mr. Schmidt's that I went to. But I keep stopping and realizing that what I know, I really don't know. I just think I know it without any facts to back me up. How's that? Am I sounding like an engineer?"

"Sounds to me like you're getting the hang of it," Jimbo said through his laughter. "Go on."

"Okay. So I decided to blog everything I know about the problems we're having."

"Wait a minute," Jimbo interrupted. "You're blogging about it? You're throwing all our dirty laundry out into the ether world for every person on the Internet to read?"

"No. No, not at all. My blogs are password protected and locked down so tight you'd have to really want to read my innermost thoughts to get in. I've been doing this since I was in high school, and I've never let anyone read a single line," Narvell explained, and not feeling the least bit guilty at what he had said since Chris hadn't read what was on this new blog yet … as far as he knew.

"Well then, why write it all down?" Jimbo looked at him with a curious expression on his face.

"It's like a diary I guess. Instead of a lock and key, it's password protected. Sounds kinda girlish when I say it that way. But it is what it is. Do you want to hear this or not? And I have a few questions for you if you'll humor me a bit."

"Go on. You got my attention."

"I'm trying to write down what it is that makes the Burdette Co. tick. How we run the company and how we measure success. I think I got a pretty good start. But, as I looked at it and rewrote most of it, I just kept coming back to the thought that everything I was writing was my opinion. So, answer me this, Jimbo. What makes M.E. Burdette Co. tick? What is the management style? What is our guiding light? How do we measure success?"

Just then their food arrived. After exchanging pleasantries with their waitress, they started eating. But Narvell wasn't about to let the topic die. "Well?"

"You really want my input on this, don't you? All right. I hope you have a good memory," Jimbo said as he lifted his fork to take another bite.

And with that Jimbo began telling Narvell his thoughts on how the company was run. His explanation became a dissertation as he went from one management topic to another. And after twenty minutes, he finally hit the subject of how the company measured success. "You've seen how we do this one. We have an incredibly complex set of metrics that measure everything in every single part of the company. I'd say in a nutshell that we leave no stone unturned. Did I just mix my metaphors?" Jimbo laughed at that thought and then suddenly jumped up from the table. "We've got to go. I've got that meeting with Fred and Bill in ten minutes. Can't be late. Bill mentioned that Fred and he have been discussing hiring someone away from Housholder. Or if that doesn't work, Bill even mentioned the idea of sending in a corporate spy. They think that whatever the boys across town are doing should be applied here. We've just got to find out what it is." And with that statement, Jimbo headed for the door.

***

Narvell spent the rest of the day thinking about what Jimbo had told him and tried to get it documented in his blog just as he had heard it. When Narvell looked at the clock on his desk his heart skipped a beat. He was late. He was supposed to pick up Annie at the airport at 5:30 and it was already 5:25. He quickly shut down his computer and headed for the parking lot.

On the drive to the airport, Narvell went over the mental list of questions he had made for Annie, including the ones he had previously blogged. He was so deep in thought, and still trying to keep his mind on his driving in the little rush hour traffic that so many locals complained about, that he almost missed the turn to the passenger terminal. As he swerved at the last second to make the turn, his cell phone rang.

"Hello."

"Narvell. Where the heck are you? I've called like 10 times. Are you coming or not?"

"Annie!" Narvell exclaimed as if he wasn't expecting her call. "I'm pulling up to the terminal now. Where are you?"

"Outside baggage claim. Hurry and get here. I'm starved."

Annie didn't even get the last sentence out when Narvell stopped the car right next to her. He popped the trunk lid and jumped out to help her with her bag.

But before he could pick up the suitcase, Annie wrapped her arms around his shoulders and gave him a hug. "Thank you, Narvell. It's nice to actually have someone pick you up when you come home."

"My pleasure," Narvell said as she let go. He then continued the task that had brought him out of the car in the first place and put her suitcase in the trunk. "What are you hungry for?"

"Well, let's see. I had pizza at Gino's East and My ∏, so that's out. I had Mexican at Frontera Grill, but that's real Mexican not Tex-Mex. And I did Bob Chinn's Crab House last night. How's a greasy ole burger sound?"

"Great. I know just the place." And with that, Narvell pulled away from the curb and headed back into town.

"Three questions for you, Narvell," Annie said as she reached over and turned down the jazz station playing on the radio. "One, why were you late? Two, what is so important that you tried calling me like every hour all morning? And three, where are we eating? No fast food, okay?"

Without hesitating, and without looking at her, Narvell answered. "I was trying to write down my thoughts and what Jimbo Chisholm told me about how our company is run. Time got away from me. Sorry." Narvell finished the statement in a very conciliatory tone, as he wound up to deliver the second answer. But first, he decided to answer question three. "We're eating at Dave's Onion Burgers, is that okay?" And without waiting for an answer, he headed into the main reason for being with Annie this evening.

"Did you hear about the meeting this morning?" Annie shook her head and waited for Narvell to continue. "Schmidt met with everyone in Engineering this morning and wants to use our department's success as a model for turning around the financial problems of the company. Bill sent out an e-mail first thing this morning and more or less threatened everyone with their jobs. Then we all played nice and said why we thought Engineering was meeting all our goals. Everyone but me, that is. Jimbo wouldn't let me talk. Cut me off and did a ten-minute dissertation. When it was all over, Jimbo sort of apologized, and I asked him how he thought Burdette was run; how we measure success. He spent quite a while explaining what he thought and then I spent the rest of the day writing in my blog trying to sort it all out."

"And … have you come to any conclusions?" Annie asked.

"Not yet. That's why we need to talk. You know I spent Friday night with Chris searching for answers, right?" Annie nodded at the statement even though Narvell was watching the road and not looking her way. "Well, Chris told me this story about a tape measure."

Annie cut him off with her laughter. "I know the story. Don't tell it to me again. I used to hear it all the time when we dated. So, now he has you looking for your tape measure, right?"

"Not exactly. After he told me the story, Chris actually offered to help me answer the questions I have in return for helping him. He is going to have to do the tape measure exercise with his grandfather at some point but won't get to use his work history since the only place he's ever worked is Housholder. So he asked me to write down everything I know about how Burdette operates; how the company is run; what the management style is, and, most importantly, how we measure success. In exchange, he'll tell me how Housholder operates. Which I think will work out great since Mr. Schmidt supposedly is interested in getting someone inside to see how they do it. I don't know why he doesn't just call them up and ask. Wouldn't that be easier?" Narvell asked rhetorically and then continued. "So I talked to Jimbo and he gave me his thoughts. I've blogged about everything I now know about the company, or to say it better, what I think I know. So, now I want to ask you some questions and then let you talk. But first, let me find a parking space and we can get a table." Narvell finished, as he turned into the parking lot at Dave's Onion Burger.

Dave's was a hole-in-the-wall burger shack on the edge of town that quite often had a line of twenty or thirty people deep outside at lunch. The ambience wasn't much; a sports theme consisting of professional football and basketball team posters mixed with autographed photos of professional athletes, movie stars, and the occasional politician that had stopped by for a burger and some fries or onion rings. Fortunately, it was a Monday evening and there were only five other customers in the restaurant. Narvell and Annie found a booth in the corner and were greeted by a waitress before they even had a chance to settle into their seats. They placed their order and then Narvell continued the conversation.

"Annie, I have several questions for you. Please don't laugh at me. Just follow me as I lay out the scenario, and then I'll ask my questions," Narvell said as he leaned forward across the table.

"Okay, I'll play. But first, you have to answer a simple question for me. Why don't you call me Bean like everyone you hung around with in college?" Annie said as she sat smiling at Narvell waiting.

"It's mean and it has always bothered me that they called you that. Any time I have called you Bean, I've felt guilty for days. And before you ask why, let me just say that if your name was Narvell it would make perfect sense to be sensitive about what names you called people. Can we continue now?" Narvell was obviously ready to learn what Annie knew, and it came through in the way he answered her question.

"Please do," she said as the smile on her face got just a little bit bigger.

"I think I told you about my looking at the big metric board by the break room. I am amazed at the amount of incredible information we have on our processes. That's part of the reason why I don't understand what the financial problems are all about. How, if every area of the company is doing so well, can we be in such trouble? And then I'm told multiple times to do as I'm told and don't rock the boat with Bill. What's up with that?

"And then to make matters worse, when I finally get an assignment of my own, Bill shuts me down when I say I can get it done in a few days. He more or less told me that it was going to take almost two weeks, regardless of what I thought. I had it done in less than two days, and that included going back over it and checking my work several times. So, now I'm waiting to turn it in. None of this makes a lot of sense to me, which is why I am actually listening to what Chris has to say. You know, underneath that goof ball facade we all saw in school, he's actually got his act together, don't you think?"

"Is that your question, Narvell? Does Chris have his act together?" Annie asked looking a bit puzzled at this odd twist in the conversation.

"No. No, not even close. I was just making an observation. I assumed you knew that. After all, you dated him for what, like two years? No, my first question is … what do you know about Bill Cooke and the way Engineering operates?"

"Narvell, I can't believe you're asking that. You're asking me how your department is run? That sounds a bit odd, doesn't it?"

"Annie, I want an outsider's perspective of what is going on. Your department asks for information and is involved in engineering projects from time to time, right?" Narvell asked as he leaned forward to take a drink of the iced tea the waitress had just set down in front of him.

"Actually, we are involved in engineering projects all the time. And the number one complaint that we hear is how long it takes to get anything out of Engineering. But the response is always the same; engineering projects are done according to the planned schedules, and it takes a certain amount of time to get it right.

"It's always the same answer. Simple requests almost always take two weeks. And they are never late. Also, I can't ever remember any request I've turned in being more than one day early. The interesting thing that some of our team who have experience at other companies have said is that it seems odd that so few schedules ever slip. How in the world does Bill keep everyone so close to the schedule? George has tried to squash the rumors around our office, but they keep popping up. The rumor is that the schedules are always strung out with lots of padding to make sure that nothing goes late. Does that help?" Annie explained and then picked up her Coke and nearly chugged the entire contents in one long sip through the straw.

"Wow. Kind of validates my thoughts on why I was told it would take almost two weeks. That helps a bunch. Does anyone ever challenge Engineering on response times given when a request is turned in or when project teams are created?"

"Are you crazy, Narvell? I don't think anyone in the company would dare cross someone at Bill's level of management. What they say goes. We are a company built on rules and following those rules and policies. Engineering has set in place a response time policy, and it is the gold standard. You saw that today when Fred met with you all wanting Engineering to help everyone else do what you all do … the on time thing, not the padding timeframes."

Narvell continued after nodding at Annie's response. "Next question … or do you want to wait until after we eat?"

Before Annie could even answer, the waitress appeared seemingly from out of nowhere with two large greasy burgers with grilled onions falling out of the buns and into the red baskets they were sitting in next to a ridiculously large mound of home-cut French fries.

Annie salted the fries and poured ketchup in the basket next to the fries. She grabbed a handful of napkins from the dispenser on the table, spread them in her lap, and looked at Narvell. "Continue. What's the next question?"

"Ooh, I just remembered something I keep meaning to tell you. Before I spring the next one on you, I've got to tell you something. We don't use the ERP system for doing costing analysis. We go pull our data from wherever we can find it, at least that's the way I interpreted it. Then we plug it all into a spreadsheet template and presto; we get our cost number. Yet, I had time to not only use Bill's, or whoever created the template, and then run the same analysis in ERP and I found a bust in the template. One big, bad calculation that has been there who knows how long. I wonder how many bad pricing decisions we've made from the bad cost figures that error has caused."

"Have you told Bill?" Annie interrupted, her voice somewhat muffled by her mouth full of hamburger.

"No. He wasn't there last week after I found it. Then today we were scrambling around dealing with the meeting and then assignments that came out of the meeting. I guess, though, I should've said something this afternoon instead of just blogging. I'll do that in the morning.

"Now, for the last question of the evening. Do you know anything about the Northeast Sales Region? I saw their metrics, and noticed a couple of things that made me think I should ask you what you know."

"Narvell, I hope you don't think the Northeast Region is up to something, too," Annie exclaimed, leaning forward with a look of concern in her voice. "Rob Allison and his team are kicking some serious ass. Rob came on board about a year and a half ago and has caught everyone in Sales and Marketing's attention. They have been beating the socks off of the other sales teams just about every month for the past year."

"Calm down. I'm not accusing anyone of anything. The fact that their numbers are so good is what caught my eye. And the weird thing is that it's the only set of metrics I've found so far on the server. I haven't found any other department or team metrics on the network server yet. Every other metric I've seen is on the Big Board. But what I think is odd is the fact that there are only three metrics … only three things. And yet, they just scream at you. So what's the deal?"

"Rob spoke at a planning retreat Marketing had a couple of months ago. He was asked that very question," Annie responded in a much lower voice, now leaning forward so Narvell could hear her. "Rob said it's the KISS principle. You know, Keep It Simple Stupid. He got verbally attacked a couple of times by other sales managers, but he stuck to his guns. He said his team understands the goals and responds. It's hard to argue with success. I do think there are some other managers who are jealous. There have been some pretty nasty things said that I've overheard as I've worked with some of the sales teams since the retreat. You can call Rob and talk to him if you want. I have his number."

"Let me write up what I know first and then talk to Chris. After that, I think I might take you up on that phone number. But for now I think I have enough to get Chris to explain how Housholder does it," Narvell said leaning back and wiping his mouth. "Man, that was a good burger."

Narvell and Annie sat and talked about her trip and then drifted off into conversation about college friends. When Annie finally looked down at her watch, she realized it was after nine o'clock. "Narv, you better get me home. I've got to unpack and do laundry before I go to bed, and I have a meeting at seven in the morning."

"Let's go," Narvell said standing up.

***

When Narvell finally got home, he headed straight for his room and turned on the computer. While it was booting up, he brushed his teeth and changed into a pair of shorts. Coming back to his desk, he sat down and logged into his blog. Without missing a beat, Narvell began typing all that he had learned from his dinner conversation, along with other thoughts that had been triggered by what Annie had said. When he was through for the night, Narvell sat and reread everything he had documented when he set up the new blog as well as his thoughts from today, both with Jimbo and Annie. After reading through the latest entry, Narvell just sat and stared at the computer screen, wondering for a long time if he was any closer to solving the mystery of M.E. Burdette Co.

Searching for Answers

Posted on **September 19, 2011**
Reply

What I originally had written on September 7ᵗʰ......

- M.E. Burdette Co. losing money?
- How much money?
- Sales is hitting their goals.
- Engineering is ahead of most milestones on both new and improved products.
- Manufacturing is beating the pants off their goals
- Every division is within budget except Transportation, most likely due to the rising price of fuel .... AGAIN!

What a day! First my head spins after sitting through my first management update meeting. Then I come home to an impromptu party and wind up revisiting my day in total. I still have no clue why M.E. Burdette Co. is losing money! Nothing has changed in five hours. However, after visiting with a former roommate at an apparently very successful company here in town, I am challenged, if not still frustrated, to find out what is going on at Burdette. In order to figure this thing out, I have been told by Chris Anselmo to find my tape measure. Actually he said "What is your tape measure." But is it mine or the company's? In order to solve the mystery, I need to:

- Figure out what my tape measure is.
- I should just go ahead and figure out the company's as well.
- Start to unravel the mystery of the loss at Burdette by understanding the way we run the company.
- DON'T JUMP TO CONCLUSIONS!!!!!!!!!!!!
- Get the right data to help in this INVESTIGATION.
- Call the Bean, if I need help.

Sounds so simple when I write it down on paper. But why is it so frustrating? Why is the answer not there? And what can Annie Gerdes, AKA the Bean, do to help. I don't even know what department she works in. Tomorrow I must look back through all the info I saw today and see what is missing. There was lots of good data on the board by the break room. I think we shall start the investigation there.

What I found about the northeast sales region......

OUTSIDE SALES – NORTHEAST REGION

UOM	BASELINE	PREVIOUS	% CHANGE	CURRENT	%CHANGE
Sales Dollars (Qtr)	374,001	479,115	28.1↑	636,899	32.9%↑
Gross Margin	27.2%	34.4%	26.5%↑	40.9%	18.9%↑
Cost of Sales (%)	27.3%	21.3%	22.0%↓	16.0%	24.9%↓

What I think I know about the company.......What I think I know about Engineering.......

- Bill Cooke runs the department like a Theory X dictator. He calls the shots and no one crosses him.
- Engineering's deadlines are all set by Bill on inflexible schedules allowing plenty of time to always finish according to schedule.
- The department's goals and objectives look stellar because no one challenges the stated response (due) date of requests submitted. Other areas of the company don't challenge the dates/timeframes provided by Engineering.
- M.E. Burdette is a company built on rules. Do the thing right. Follow the rules.
- Success is measured at the department level. Each department has its own set of metrics that they live and die by. There are more than three or four hundred metrics listed on the Big Board outside the break room for everyone to see. Some areas easily have more than 100 different things they measure.
- The Northeast Sales Region ONLY show 3 measures on the Big Board: sales dollars; margin; and cost of sales. And yet, they are the best sales team in the company in spite of having the fewest metrics. Why???
- Jimbo has said that the secret to success and a long career is to keep your mouth shut and follow the rules.
- We are a company built on rules and policies. Follow the rules!
- Jimbo mentioned that Bill said management was considering hiring away someone from Housholder, or might try to send in a plant to spy on their methods (probably shouldn't tell anyone this).
- Success is based upon in-depth analysis and extremely detailed metrics that measures almost every process in the company.
- Management is grown from within (see above from Jimbo re: long careers).
- Jimbo also gave me a lot more info , but I think it is just his personal philosophy at this point. Maybe I can discuss some with Chris?

All right Mr. Anselmo, it is now your turn. What about Housholder???

Posted in Blogs from the book | Leave a reply

Chapter 7

Just Follow the Rules

September 20

Tuesday morning, Narvell woke up feeling refreshed for the first time in nearly two weeks. It was as if his blogging the night before had purged all the worries that had been pent up inside him since that first meeting with Fred Schmidt and the engineers and managers. Narvell actually thought about how the monkey was off his back and now it was on Chris' as he drove to work.

The first thing he did when he got to the office was to send Chris an e-mail announcing that he had finished his exercise. Now it was Chris' turn to critique his work and explain the way Housholder operated. After sending the e-mail, he headed down the hall to the copy room where the coffee pot was located. As he walked through the department, he noticed that there were not many staff members around. After pouring himself a cup of coffee, he checked to see if there was any mail in his mail slot on the far wall of the copy room and then headed back to his cubicle. That's when he noticed the conference room.

As he walked by, the door opened and several engineers came out with a look of genuine fear on their faces. They glanced his way, but said nothing before turning and heading off towards the other end of the department. Before the door closed, Narvell caught a view of what appeared to be eight or ten engineers sitting at the conference table. At the far end he could make out Bill Cooke sitting forward in his chair speaking in what sounded like an agitated voice, yet it wasn't loud enough for Narvell to make out what he was saying. Then the door was closed again.

Narvell remembered that he still had not discussed the formula error in the costing template, so he typed an e-mail to Bill explaining the problem and asking him if he would be available to discuss the issue today. After hitting the **Send** button, Narvell got up and headed for the Big Board by the break room. Since he really didn't have much more to do until he could meet with Bill about the error or turn in his costing assignment, he decided the best use of his time would be to explore the metrics once more. But this time he had an idea.

When he arrived at the Big Board, Narvell immediately started to review all the metrics from each sales team to see what was different from the Northeast Region. While each and every team had overall sales and margin reported, none of the other teams had cost of sales listed. Additionally, he noticed that all the other teams had multiple measurements for each team member. Narvell found a napkin lying on the floor under the Big Board and picked it up. Taking the pen that was hanging from a buttonhole on his shirt, he began to write on the napkin—making a list of what things were being measured by Sales for each sales representative. When he was through, he scanned the list to make sure everything on the board was written down.

Metric	*Goal*	*Actual*
– Phone calls	✗	✗
– Emails	✗	✗
– In-person calls	✗	✗
– Time spent on calls		✗
– Top line movement	✗	✗
– # of cold calls		✗
– # of warm calls		✗
– # of appointments	✗	✗
– Single line sales		✗
– Multiline contracts		✗
– # of presentations w/ buyers		✗
– # of presentations w/ C.O. level		✗

As Narvell looked over the list, what he thought was the most interesting was that there were seven items being measured that had no goals—just actual results. Then as he reread the list for the third time, he began to ask himself what several of the items actually had to do with a sales team being successful. Narvell made a mental note to ask both Chris and Annie what they thought about this topic.

Narvell then went back to his cubicle to see if Chris had seen his e-mail, or perhaps even if Bill might be free and could discuss the formula problem.

However, the only e-mail in his inbox was a follow up from Staci in Purchasing. She had resent all the information that he had already received on the cost of the fastener he had asked her about. The only difference was this time there was a receipt request attached. Narvell checked the **Ok** button to send the response to Staci and then deleted the e-mail.

Just as Narvell started to pull up his blog, Bill appeared at the opening to his cubicle. "Narvell, come to my office. I believe we have something to discuss." And without waiting for an answer, Bill turned and walked away. Narvell leapt from his chair and quickly followed Bill down the hall. This was his chance to impress the boss. He had found an error in the costing formula and he was about to explain it to Bill. He could hardly contain himself as he walked into Bill's office.

"I saw your e-mail. So, you think you found an error in our costing formula. Explain. And just give me the facts. I have a meeting in minutes," Bill said as he sat down.

"Yes, sir. When I was reviewing the calculations for the cost assignment you gave me, I found where overhead dollars being applied for purchased parts is being subtracted from the purchase price instead of being added. I checked every purchased component part in my analysis, and it was done the same way on every part," Narvell explained with just a hint of satisfaction in his voice.

Bill looked at Narvell and then looked at the e-mail Narvell had sent him, then back at Narvell. "Did you show the overhead as a negative or positive number?" Bill asked.

"Positive. Why would I show it as a negative?"

"Because we have always shown it as a negative number. Didn't you read the instructions page, son?"

"No, sir. I didn't see an instructions page. I'll go look right now. But can I ask you one question?" Narvell asked as the confidence began to drain from his body. Without waiting for Bill's answer, he continued. "Why do we not use the costing module in the ERP system? It gave me almost the same exact values, except for the error, er, uh, the negative-positive overhead value. Wouldn't using the ERP module be easier?"

"First of all, Narvell, you need to understand how the system works. We use the prescribed policies of the company to complete all of our tasks. That is how we know that we did it right. I thought we'd already had this discussion. Second, the costing module in ERP has not been approved by the management team for use. If, or when, that happens, I will make the appropriate changes to our policies and procedures and then, and only then, will you be authorized to deviate from the current practice. I cannot make this any clearer. Our structure and adherence to this structure is what makes M.E. Burdette what it is. Is that clear?" Bill asked, standing up and leaning towards Narvell for emphasis. "I don't want to have this conversation again." And with that, Bill walked out of his office and down the hall towards the conference room.

Narvell just sat there, stunned. Not sure what to do. Not sure, whether he was right or wrong. So, he just sat there for a full five minutes. Finally, he got up from the chair he had been sitting in and slowly walked back to his cubicle.

Pulling up the costing template, Narvell looked at each tab within the spreadsheet and could not find any instructions that even remotely suggested that you should enter any number as a negative. He read the instruction section that covered overhead three times just to make sure that he wasn't missing anything. When he was satisfied that he had done nothing wrong, he closed the file.

Pulling up his web browser, Narvell navigated to his blog. Logging in, he checked to see if Chris had responded yet to his part of the assignment. Nothing yet. Narvell thought about calling Chris, but then decided against it. He would give him until the end of the day and then call him tonight if he still hadn't added his information.

Narvell began to think about what his next move would be when he realized that he had not turned in the cost analysis project yet. He clicked through the menu structure on the company intranet site and quickly arrived at the folder where his project was stored. He opened the file and made the one change necessary to report the overhead amount *correctly*. He then saved the file and copied it so he could send it to Bill. Opening his e-mail program, Narvell then typed a short message that simply said, "Here is the requested cost analysis for Sales. Please let me know if there is anything else I need to do for this project." Attaching the file to the e-mail, Narvell then sent it to Bill.

Now what? He had just turned in his assignment formatted the way Bill had instructed, and now he had absolutely nothing to do. Deciding that pushing Chris a bit might not be such a bad thing, Narvell popped up his e-mail one more time and fired off a quick note to Chris asking if he had seen his blog with the Burdette information yet. After that, Narvell decided to send an e-mail to Annie as well asking if she was doing anything after work.

Just as he hit the **Send** button on his e-mail to Annie, Narvell noticed that he had a reply from Chris. Clicking on his inbox, Narvell saw the words he was looking for: "Got your information … thanks. You've done your part and now so have I. When do you want to get together to talk?"

Quickly Narvell pulled up his Web browser and logged into his blog with a great feeling of excitement. He was finally going to see what Chris had to say about Housholder, and he would be able to compare the two companies. Suddenly, Narvell felt like he had the answers in sight. He skipped over his initial thoughts and went straight to the section about what he thought he knew about Engineering. Chris had reformatted this section to make it easier to compare. For the next half hour, Narvell read and reread both his and Chris' thoughts and opinions about their two companies.

A Comparison of Companies

Posted on **September 20, 2011**
Reply

Not bad for a first shot out of the box, Narvell. As you can see I tried to align my answers up with yours. I hope this helps you in your search for the answers. Let's get together Friday night for dinner. I'll pick you up after work at your house. In the meantime, I strongly suggest you call the Sales Manager in the Northeast Region and ask him why he does what he does.

-Chris-

What I think I know about Engineering (Burdette)	What Chris thinks he knows about Housholder Engineering
• Bill Cooke runs the department like a Theory X dictator. He calls the shots and no one crosses him.	• Theory Y through and through. Engineers are given the freedom to succeed.
• Engineering's deadlines are all set by Bill on inflexible schedules allowing plenty of time to always finish according to schedule.	• Deadlines are established by the project team for each project based upon complexity of the project.
• The department's goals and objectives look stellar because no one challenges the stated response (due) date of requests submitted. Other areas of the company don't challenge the dates / timeframes provided by Engineering.	• Housholder Engineering's goals are simple: Did we get the project done in time to satisfy our customer.
What I think I know about the company.......	**What Chris knows is different about Housholder Sprockets**
• M.E. Burdette is a company built on rules. Do the thing right. Follow the rules.	• Housholder is a company built on ethics and doing the right things.
• Success is measured at the department level. Each department has its own set of metrics that they live and die by. There are more than three or four hundred metrics listed on the Big Board outside the break room for everyone to see. Some areas easily have more than 100 different things	• Success is measured with your tape measure: a few simple metrics that have great meaning to the employees on the team. The only rule is that they must, in some way, support the metrics above them in the organizational chart.
	• Have you asked this manager why he

they measure.

- The Northeast Sales Region ONLY measures 3 things: sales dollars; margin; and cost of sales. And yet, they are the best sales team in the company in spite of having the fewest metrics. Why???

- Jimbo has said that the secret to success and a long career is to keep your mouth shut and follow the rules.

- We are a company built on rules and policies. Follow the rules!

- Jimbo mentioned that Bill said management was considering hiring away someone from Housholder, or might try to send in a plant to spy on their methods (probably shouldn't tell anyone this).

- Success is based upon in-depth analysis and extremely detailed metrics that measures almost every process in the company.

- Management is grown from within (see above from Jimbo re: long careers).

- Jimbo also gave me a lot more info , but I think it is just his personal philosophy at this point. Maybe I can discuss some with Chris?

only has 3? Maybe he has found his tape measure.

- If any manager said that at Housholder they would be shown the door. We need to hear what everyone thinks and knows; ALL THE TIME!

- Rules again! We have rules, and we are interested in doing both the right things and in doing things right.

- Why would you need to do that? All you have to do is ask. Our company routinely holds executive roundtables to discuss what companies are doing both right and wrong. We've even had competition from within our own industry come a time or two.

- Success is ultimately measured by the KPIs of the company; those few things that our CEO and executive management agree are the true tape measure of success.

- While our goal is always to grow from within, sometimes you just don't have the horses (my father said that).

- Jimbo sounds pretty smart, if not a bit cautious. Maybe we can both talk to him.

Posted in Blogs from the book | Leave a reply

Chapter 8

Don't Rock the Boat

"Okay, everyone. In the conference room. Now!" Narvell sat straight up in his chair when he heard the booming voice announce this. Bill was walking through Engineering telling everyone to go to the conference room. Narvell had only been back from lunch for a few minutes, so it wasn't like he was being distracted from any work by this command. He did, however, begin to wonder what could have taken place during the hour he was out of the office.

So, Narvell gathered a pad of paper and a pencil and headed for his now customary seat against the wall in the engineering conference room. Sitting down, he noticed that neither Bill nor Jimbo looked very happy. As he looked around the room, Narvell saw that several of the other engineering managers and senior engineers had this same unhappy expression. And then, in walked Fred Schmidt. Fred had the same expression on his face only he was staring straight at Bill as if he were trying to burn holes in the engineering director's body.

Walking up to the head of the table next to where Bill was seated, Fred began to speak without hesitation. "People, I am not going to mince words here. We are in trouble as a company. I asked you all for ideas on how to turn around the financial problem we are having. What I didn't expect is that the plan Engineering would deliver would identify what was wrong, specifically. Bill and his team have stated, but I'm not convinced yet, that the problem is that many parts of the company just do not live up to the policies, procedures, and processes that have run this company for years. Bill did correctly note that parts of the company that do not meet their deadlines throw the entire company into chaos. It puts undue pressure on everything that happens next. But, this does not, in my opinion or that of the board, explain everything. This company is supposed to be engineering driven and customer focused. Well, we can't go ask our customers why we are losing money, but we can ask you all—the engineers. So, in order for me to take Bill's plan to the board, I need you all to tell me what you know, believe, think, or feel is contributing to our problems. So, get started. We're not leaving the room until I'm satisfied that we know what to go work on."

As Fred was addressing the engineering staff, Narvell noticed that people seemed to be trickling into the room and finding seats. He recognized several as vice presidents and directors, but the majority of the people were new faces to Narvell. When no one spoke up immediately, Fred continued on. "I've asked a few other management team members from around the company to join us. They're not here to defend their work any more than you all are. We all just want to find out where the problem is. Now, speak up. Any thoughts?"

"Yes, sir. I'll go first," one of the product engineers said. "It seems to me from where we sit in R&D that we continue to generate new products, but nothing ever happens. We never hear of 80% of the new products being sold or even marketed for that matter. Why doesn't Sales and Marketing do their jobs?"

Allyson, who had come in late and had not found a seat yet, immediately turned towards the engineer seated at the table who had made the remark. "When you all invent something that Marketing can market and that Sales can sell, then we'll sell it. The reason why you only see 20% of your work go to market is because the other 80% is crap." Her response was raw with emotion and the look on her face showed how annoyed she was with the engineer and his comments.

"Hold on, Allyson," said Fred as he stepped in between Allyson and the engineer. "I just said that this was not about defending one position or the other. You may not agree with what is being said, but if that is the perception, then it is what it is. Now sit down and let's continue.

"We need to know what the problem is and we need a plan to fix it. Bill's plan may be the answer, but we need to know what the problem is as well. I've talked to Bill and several other directors and managers about some options. We're looking at trying to hire away some key employees from Housholder Sprockets and Culbert Implement Co. For those of you who do not know, these two manufacturers here in the area have a track record of posting profits almost every year since they were started. Neither company has lost money in the last twenty years. The board has been talking about injecting some new blood into our system. That may not be such a bad idea.

It was even discussed that maybe we should *let* one of our finance staff members 'get hired away' by one of those companies to get someone on the inside to see how they are doing it." Fred raised both arms in the air and made quote signs with his fingers to get his message across about letting someone get hired away.

Jimbo looked at Narvell when Fred made this remark and Narvell nodded to acknowledge what Jimbo had told him already. Then suddenly Jimbo looked up at Fred and said, "Fred, isn't it possible that our problems are based in synchronization, or rather the lack thereof, of the various parts of the company?"

"What do you mean, Jimbo? Explain please."

"Well, perhaps we are all doing things right, but just not at the right time. Maybe we need to reset ourselves as an organization."

"Hmmm. Hadn't considered that, Jimbo. We ought to look into that," Fred said as he wrote the word *synchronization* on the white board on the wall where Jimbo and Narvell were seated. "Other thoughts?"

Narvell sat and looked around the now silent room for what seemed like an eternity, but was actually closer to fifteen or twenty seconds, before speaking up. "Sir, I've only been here for a few weeks, so I may be way off base here. But listening to what Jimbo said and from some things I've noticed about the metrics board by the break room, I was wondering if maybe we aren't measuring the wrong stuff." Narvell realized what he was saying only after he said it, and then immediately began to search for the right words to make sure he didn't say anything that would be taken wrong. "What I mean is …. Well, we seem to be measuring a lot of things … that we do … but, are we measuring what others do? Er, … what I mean is … in college we learned to observe what you do as a company … what your competition does … and, what other companies in general are doing … both good and bad."

Narvell started to say something about his costing project and the required timeframe Bill had given him. But, just as he opened his mouth, Jimbo chimed in: "Narvell, I understand what you are saying. But, all of our competition holds their financial details very close to the chest. None of them are publicly traded, so how do we observe them if we can't get close?"

Narvell hadn't expected that statement, especially from Jimbo. Just as he started to answer, Fred said, "Son, Narvell is it? That is a very interesting thought. But I have to agree with Jimbo. It's a tough industry we're in. But you could be right about doing a better job observing what others in the area are doing both right and wrong. Thank you." And with a wry-looking smile on his face and a nod of his head, Fred wrote *Observe others* on the board. Narvell thought that the look on Mr. Schmidt's face seemed to take Narvell's comments as an endorsement of the idea to place spies into other companies.

After Fred's public display of appreciation for Narvell's comments, it was like the floodgates had opened. Several other of the younger engineers spoke up and questioned why they always seemed to reinvent the wheel with every project. One of the sales managers who had come in with Allyson then brought up the concern that there never seemed to be communication about any project taking place, whether it be an engineering, marketing, IT, or even a sales initiative. It just seemed like people were working in a vacuum. At that comment, Fred wrote COMMUNICATION! on the board.

As the discussion was winding down, Jimbo nudged Narvell and motioned towards Bill with his hand still on his lap, so no one at the table could see what he was doing. When Narvell looked over at Bill, a knot quickly formed in his stomach. Bill's face had turned red and he was staring at each person as they spoke. Suddenly, he turned towards Jimbo and Narvell and locked eyes with Narvell. His stare was so unsettling that Narvell could not look back, and not being able to leave, all he could do was look away. When Bill finally looked back at the person that was now speaking, Jimbo leaned towards Narvell. "Someone is pissed at one of us, Narv. For your sake, you better hope he's mad at me for starting this dialog."

When Fred decided that he had heard enough, he politely brought the meeting to an end and thanked everyone. "We have what appears to be a list of things to look at for possible solutions. Thanks everyone. The exec team will have each of these ideas studied in greater depth." And with a dismissive wave of his hand, everyone began to stand and exit the room.

Jimbo stood and turned his back on Bill so he could talk to Narvell. "Narv, if I were you, I'd steer clear of Bill for a few days. Let me take the heat on this one. He may be mad at me for what I said. Not sure which of us tripped his trigger, but I'll get into his office and defuse him. The smart thing would be to leave the room and go straight down to the break room and buy a pop. Sip on it slowly just in case, okay?"

"Thanks, Jimbo. Who do you really think Bill is upset with … you … or me?"

"You. I've seen the look before. He rarely comes unglued at the old timers. It's usually the new kid that steps in it in Bill's eyes. Just go downstairs and let me handle this so you don't have to suffer through this. He'll calm down by tomorrow."

With the message now loud and clear from Jimbo, Narvell headed for the door. As he was walking down the hall towards the stairwell, he heard a voice behind him. "Narvell, right? Interesting name you got there. Rob Allison, Sales. Nice to meet you," said the man walking up beside Narvell as he stuck out his hand to shake Narvell's. "I liked what you said in there. That took some guts from what I've been told about your boss. He's one tough S.O.B. isn't he?"

"Narvell Mann. Nice to meet you, Rob. Hey, aren't you the sales manager for the Northeast Region?"

"I am. How'd you know that? You study the org chart for fun?"

"No, actually I'm a college friend of Annie Gerdes in Marketing. I noticed your metrics on the server and was asking Annie about them. She's pretty impressed with what your team is doing; not that that really matters, I guess."

"Well, thanks for the kind words. And I'll have to remember to thank Annie as well. I am dead serious when I say I liked what you said to Fred. Maybe someone will start listening if enough of us continue to talk about these things. It didn't look like Bill was too happy with you or Jimbo by the end. I was watching him most of the meeting, and it really looked like he wasn't happy about anyone's comments though. I do wish someone at the top would understand how important it is to observe what others are doing, in and out of industry. And, you don't have to resort to corporate espionage to do it. I wonder if anyone on the exec team ever thought about reading the business section of the newspaper?" With that comment, Rob started laughing. "Oh, I crack myself up sometimes. Sorry, Narvell. Where you headed?"

"Down to the break room to get something to drink. And you?" Narvell responded politely, not sure where this conversation was headed.

"I've got a meeting with Allyson, and then I'm headed to the airport. Gotta get back to my team. They need their number-one cheerleader to keep encouraging them. We're on track for another record quarter. One last question, why were you asking Annie about our region's numbers?"

"That's simple. (A) They are so good, and (B) because there are only three metrics. It caught my eye as to how easy and yet powerful those metrics appeared."

"Okay. Thanks for another compliment. If you're ever up in the Northeast, drop in and see us. Good luck." And with that, Rob turned and headed towards the front of the building, as Narvell stepped into the stairwell and headed down to the break room. But before he could get to the first landing going down the stairs, he heard a commotion above him. It sounded like it was coming from the hall where he had just left. He stopped dead in his tracks when he heard his name.

"I don't give a crap what you or that little pissant think, Jimbo. What the hell did you two think you were doing?" Narvell heard Bill say in a voice that was almost a shout from the doorway on the landing above him. "I had this under control. I had a plan and all any one of you needed to say was that Engineering is running smoothly. But did you? No, instead you want to talk about synchronization and that Narvell puke wants to talk about college and observing others. If you don't shut that kid up, I will. Understand?" Bill's voice was now loud enough that other employees who had been heading up the stairs from the first floor had heard it and turned around and headed back out into the first floor hallway.

Narvell quickly walked down the stairs and towards the break room. His legs were shaking with each step, and as he walked through the break room door, he realized that his hands were shaking as well. He walked over to a pop machine, put a dollar into the slot and pushed the top button on the selection panel without even looking to see what it was. He grabbed the bottle of pop and sat down at the first table to compose himself. As he was sitting there, two employees he recognized from the meeting, but had no idea who they were, walked up to him. "Narvell. That was some meeting, wasn't it? We liked what all of you guys that spoke up had to say. You going to stay down here until the smoke clears upstairs?" the one closest to Narvell said.

"I probably should. Jimbo sent me down here to avoid Bill. From what I heard on my way down, it sounds like Jimbo was right," Narvell said as he stared straight through his soft drink.

The other person leaned in close and said, "You may want to just sneak out the door and head for home. When we ducked down the stairs, it was getting close to a full-scale war up there. Bill was yelling at Jimbo and Paula, along with two of the other engineers that spoke up. Allyson stepped in on her way back to her office and tried to break it up, and Bill started in on her. It was not a pretty sight. Not the first time that's happened, though. You got anything you can do out on the manufacturing floor? If not, you may want to make something up." And with that, the two turned and headed across the room.

Twenty minutes later, Narvell looked up from the table and saw Jimbo walking in the break room. He came straight over to Narvell and sat down. "Okay it's safe to come out of hiding. Bill's gone for the rest of the day. Said he had an offsite meeting. You okay?"

"Am I okay? What about you? You were the one up there with Bill in your face. Holy cow! And the amazing thing to me is that no one that has come through here since the shouting started seems to think anything about it. What the heck?"

"Look, Narv. It's Bill. What can I say? Things will be better tomorrow. Come on. Let's get back to work," Jimbo said, standing back up. Narvell stood up with him and as they headed out the door and back up to Engineering, Narvell noticed that his whole body was still shaking a bit.

When Narvell got back to his cubicle, he sat down and logged into his computer. Pulling up his Web browser, he quickly navigated to his blog, logged in and began typing.

Questioning the Whole Thing!

Posted on **September 20, 2011**
Reply

What have I gotten myself into? Am I working for a madman? What started out, I thought, as a very productive meeting to address our company problems turned into a shouting match in the hall. Jimbo took more than a bullet for me on this. I owe him big time.

But did I learn anything from the meeting?

Jimbo asked if the company was synchronized.

I asked if we were observing what other companies are doing. Mr. Schmidt seemed to take my comment as backing his spy idea. Not what I meant!

Communication was another big buzz word. We apparently are not communicating very well. Duh? That was pretty obvious from the shouting match, wasn't it?

I did meet Rob Allison, though. Maybe I'll call him and talk about this. He might have some ideas.

Posted in Blogs from the book | Leave a reply

Chapter 9

Asking the Right Questions

Just before Narvell had left the office Tuesday evening, Chris had called and left Narvell a message on his cell phone canceling their dinner that night, which did not bother Narvell in the least. He was totally drained from the afternoon's excitement and just wanted to go home and decompress in peace and quiet. Wednesday morning Jimbo had stopped by and told Narvell that Bill and the exec team would be offsite the rest of the week discussing Tuesday afternoon's meeting.

Annie called and checked on him Wednesday night. Narvell still didn't want to talk about it. Annie even offered to buy him dinner, but it was not to be. Narvell was determined to suffer alone. Before Annie hung up, she did get Narvell to agree to dinner Friday evening. He agreed on the condition that they include Chris. Annie agreed and said she would call Chris and set it up.

So now it was Friday and Narvell went through the day in a nervous haze just waiting for Bill to reappear and unload on him like he had done to Jimbo. When Narvell came back from lunch, he saw that Bill's office lights were on, but he never saw Bill. Jimbo stopped by mid-afternoon and told him that the crisis was over, and that Bill had moved on to other more important things. When Narvell asked what was more important than the company's bottom line, Jimbo responded that engineering projects were always the most important thing in the world to Bill. At that comment, Narvell could feel himself relax a little.

Just before 5:00 p.m., Annie appeared from nowhere staring over the cubicle wall at Narvell and his completely empty desk. "Hey, big guy. Do you work here?" she said with a laugh.

"No. I'm just here to make sure no one else can use this cubicle. Are you a new employee? I don't believe I've seen you around here," Narvell teased back at her, feeling better just seeing her smiling face. "You ready to go get some dinner?"

"You bet, Narvell. You know me. I'll always eat. I talked to Chris and he's going to meet us. Let's go," Annie said as she turned and headed for the door.

When they got to the parking lot, Annie grabbed Narvell by the arm. "Ride with me, Narv. We can come back after dinner and get your car." Narvell didn't argue. He climbed in the passenger seat of Annie's incredibly small subcompact convertible and slid the seat back.

"Maybe we should take my car. There's definitely more leg room. Whaddaya say, Annie?"

"Nope. I'm the chauffeur tonight. Sit back and relax. I promise to get you there in one piece," Annie replied as she accelerated hard out of the parking lot and out onto the highway in front of M.E. Burdette Co.

Fifteen minutes later Annie turned off the highway and headed down a tree-lined street. The sun was casting shadows across the road, and Narvell suddenly realized he had no idea where they were eating. He hadn't really been paying attention up to now, but the flashing in and out of the shadows brought him back to the moment. "Where are we going? I didn't know there were any restaurants out on this side of town," Narvell said looking over at Annie. He noticed she had a grin on her face and for some reason the nervous anticipation he had experienced most of the week suddenly returned.

"We're meeting Chris at his parent's house for burgers. Chris thought you might like a bit of peace and quiet in a laid-back setting. If you want to talk about what happened this week, we'll both listen. If not, we'll just eat, drink some beer and get silly. Is that okay?" Annie's tone changed and became very soft with the last sentence. She looked over at Narvell with what seemed to him to be one of concern and compassion.

"Sure. It might be nice to just kick back with you guys this evening. Thanks." And just as though the entire conversation had been orchestrated, Annie made a quick right turn just as Narvell finished his sentence. Pulling into the neighborhood, Annie drove down the main street, turned left and headed towards the driveway at the far end of the street. As she turned into the long drive, both of them saw Chris climb out of his car and walk up to the front door.

When Chris heard Annie's car pulling in, he turned and waved. But, instead of waiting for them on the porch, Chris opened the door and went inside, closing the door behind him. "He sure doesn't act like he was expecting us, Annie. What gives?"

"Nothing. Chris used to do that when we were dating. Any time we would meet out here or if I followed him in my car, he would always run to the front door, go in and close the door behind him. Then his mother would come to the door and open it when I rang the doorbell, and give me a big hug before I could go in. You better get ready."

Sure enough, as soon as Narvell and Annie stepped onto the porch, the door swung open and out stepped Chris' mother. She immediately grabbed Annie in a hug and squeezed her for a full thirty seconds, then let go and stepped back saying, "Annie, you look fantastic. It's a shame my son was such a boob. He really should have stopped his partying and let you make an honest man out of him. Oh well, his loss. So, is this your new beau?"

Annie looked over at Narvell and blushed. Before she could say anything, Mrs. Anselmo had Narvell in a hug. Narvell thought she would suffocate him before she finally let go. "Young man, welcome to our home. I'm Sharon Anselmo. And you are?"

"Narvell, Narvell T. Mann, Mrs. Anselmo. It's a pleasure to finally meet you."

At that pronouncement, Sharon stopped dead in her tracks and stared at Narvell. Finally, she said, "I know that name. You roomed with Chris one year in college, right? I thought he made you up. He never brought you home. I never saw him with you when we were on campus. Wow. You really do exist. Now, quit being so proper. If you will tell me what the "T" stands for, you can quit calling me Mrs. Anselmo, just call me Sharon."

"Actually ma'am, I'd rather just call you Mrs. Anselmo."

"No, you don't. It's Sharon. We are not that formal around here. Understand?"

"It's not you, it's me. I'm not real thrilled with my middle name. I hope you don't mind?"

"Not at all, son. Come on in. Chris and his father are out back. Annie, you know the way. Have fun." Sharon waved them through and headed up the staircase just inside the front door.

Annie led the way through the living room and past the formal dining room before turning through a door into the family room. Crossing the room, she opened the French doors on the outside of the room and they walked out onto the deck. Sitting in Adirondack chairs next to the gas grill and facing the expansive back yard were Chris and his father. Annie walked up to the chairs and placed a hand on the shoulder of the elder Anselmo. "Hi, Mr. A. Did you miss me?" she said and laughed as if there was a secret joke between the two of them. Mr. Anslemo stood up and grabbed Annie by the hand. "Annie, my dear. I always miss you." Then he turned towards his son and said, "Shmuck."

Chris looked over at Narvell. "Can you tell my parents weren't exactly thrilled about us breaking up?" At that comment, everyone laughed. "Grab a beer, Narv. They're in the refrigerator over by the sink."

Before Narvell could even turn to see where the sink and refrigerator were, Annie was already across the deck opening the refrigerator and grabbing a couple of beers for them. Coming back over, she motioned him to the other two chairs sitting at a right angle to the ones the Anselmos were standing by. "Narvell, Tom Anselmo. Nice to meet you," Mr. Anselmo said as he stuck out a hand.

"Nice to meet you, sir. I've heard a lot about you from Chris."

"Hope it's not all bad," Tom said as the two of them shook hands.

As they all sat down, Chris explained the menu for the evening. "Dad is graciously serving as our chef tonight. He is currently grilling stuffed poblano peppers. While the burgers are cooking, we can munch on the peppers. After we have our burgers with chips and baked beans, Mom has made us a lemonade icebox pie. You'd better like it. Er, I mean I hope you like it. She's very proud of her desserts."

***

After dinner, Chris and his parents along with Narvell and Annie were seated around the table on the deck eating their pie when Chris first brought up the subject. "Narv, you want to talk about what happened this week? I saw your rather short blog entries Tuesday night and Wednesday night. Rough week, huh?"

"Not really, no. Bill is an ass. Excuse my language, Mrs. Anselmo. But he is."

"For the umpteenth time Narvell, it is Sharon. I warned you last time: If you called me Mrs. Anselmo one more time, you would have to tell me your middle name. You agreed. So now, you can keep your word. Spit it out."

Before Narvell could even open his mouth, Chris and Annie had already begun to snicker. "Both of you, zip it," Narvell hissed glaring at the two of them.

Annie replied, "But Narv, we know where this is going. It always happens." And she started laughing.

"Sharon, my middle name is *The*." Narvell said with a very serious look on his face.

"What?"

"The. Like *Theo* without the *O*."

"Isn't Theo short for Theodore?" Sharon asked with a confused expression on her face.

"Yes ma'am. And The is short for Theo. That's what my mom says. My middle name comes from Theodore Roosevelt. My mom said that her grandfather used to tell her stories about Teddy Roosevelt and the Rough Riders. Only he always called him Theo, not Teddy. I don't know why. So, Mom decided to shorten Theo to The. Once again, I don't know why. So, don't even ask me. There it is, Narvell The Mann." Amazingly enough, Narvell told this with a deadpan expression on his face while Annie and Chris were both lying on the deck laughing.

Sharon looked at them when Narvell had finished and asked, "What is so funny, you two?"

All Chris could say was, "Narvell, you're *the* man." And then he was laughing again.

"It's okay Sharon. Every time I explain where my name comes from, they do this. It's not just them. I've heard it all my life. Tomorrow, they'll both feel bad about it and buy my lunch or a beer or something. It's all good. Okay, you two, joke's over. Let's move on to other stories, shall we?"

"Okay, sorry Narv. Now, will you please explain the week to us?" Chris said, almost begging Narvell to talk. "Annie tried to explain to me last night what all happened at work, but she said she thought it was nothing but a bunch of rumors."

"No, I didn't. I said I got it third hand, so it was mostly hearsay. You still don't listen to me, do you, Chris?"

"Okay. Okay. I'll talk if it keeps you two from fighting about it," Narvell injected into the middle of their conversation.

Narvell then spent the next ten minutes recalling the events of the week, starting with the meeting and Bill's reaction to what he and Jimbo had said, and ending with the odd silence that fell over the office as the week progressed. When he was finished, it was Tom Anselmo, and not Chris, who spoke first. "I hate to say anything bad about another human being, but this Bill fellow sounds like an absolute jerk. Now I know there are two sides to every story, so let me ask you a question. How did you and … Jimbo is it? How did you two say your comments? Were you respectful with what you said, or were you flippant or condescending in any way?"

"Oh, no, sir. I thought that I was quite respectful in how I talked. After all, I'm the new guy. I may be young, but I don't think I'm that stupid. And Jimbo was incredibly polite in his comments. I thought he was actually trying to throw a life preserver out for everyone to kind of grab hold of. I think this whole thing goes right along with the way Bill runs the department—his way or the highway. I guess what Jimbo and I said put us on the highway out of town until Jimbo calmed Bill down. Of course, I still haven't seen him since he blew up."

"Narvell, if you don't mind, I'd like to hear more about this. If any of you have a problem with it, just tell me to get lost," Tom said looking around at all three of them. In response, both Annie and Chris turned towards Narvell.

"Narvie, your call. After all it's your problem," Annie said softly as she reached out and touched his forearm.

"I guess I don't have anything to lose at this point, sir. And if I can figure it all out, maybe I can keep my job. Of course I am beginning to wonder if I want to," Narvell said, then emitted a nervous laugh as he nodded at Tom.

"All right then. Can I ask you a few questions?"

"Sure. Go right ahead."

"Okay. First things, first. Chris told me he explained the tape measure. Do you understand what the story means?"

"Sort of. But the more I think about it, the more unsure of myself I am as I look for answers."

"All right. Honesty. I like that. Did Chris talk to you about the human side of the story? In other words, did he talk about the people aspect or just the measurement piece?"

"I think it was just the measurement piece, Mr. Anselmo. But I could be wrong."

"Well then, let's go there. Who are the leaders at M.E. Burdette, Narvell?"

"Our president, of course, Fred Schmidt. Then there's the management team; Bill, my boss, and Allyson the VP of Sales, and ..." Before Narvell could finish, Tom interrupted. "Not who are your managers, who are your leaders? Who are the people that your employees follow? Who are those people that others turn to for direction, for support, and even for comfort when something goes wrong?"

"Oh. I don't think I've looked at it that way before. I would definitely say Bill and Allyson are *not*. I really don't know, Mr. Schmidt, and I have no idea how he works with the management team. I would say though that Jimbo is a leader in Engineering. He ran interference for me with Bill this week. And he seems to be the guy that everyone in Engineering turns to for answers and direction after Bill has barked out his orders. I'm still fairly new, so I don't know a lot of people yet. But, based on what Annie has said, I would think that Rob Allison, one of the sales managers, is a leader. He has done amazing things with his region's sales numbers. Even though I've only met him once, he talked about the team effort and even said I could call him and ask questions if I wanted."

"That's good, son. Think about this topic some more over the next few days or weeks. Watch those around you. Try to *see* the leaders. They are usually fairly easy to identify once you start looking. Next question: How do employees respond to the boss? In other words, do employees eagerly jump into assignments when given them by their supervisors? Or do they shuffle through the day, or maybe even go talk to the Jimbos of the world to get clarification or reassurance? This also can help you with the leader versus manager issue."

Narvell thought about this one and then said, "I can only speak for Engineering on this one. I would say we have a mixture. There're one or two that seem to jump when Bill speaks. But, I think they are more of suck-ups than anything else. About half our staff seems to talk to Jimbo just about every day. Many of the questions I've heard when I'm with him are pretty simple. Like you said, almost as if they are getting reassurances before they stick their necks out. Annie, what's it like in Marketing?"

"George is a good manager, and yes, I view him as a leader. He tries to carry the company line, but he does let us know when he has a different opinion. He is constantly reminding us to focus on who our customers are and why we exist as a team or department. And Tom, to answer your question about how people respond, I'd have to say that just about everyone on the team are on board. Most of us are excited about our jobs and feel like we get very good direction and support from George. I hope that makes him a good leader. I sure look up to him. But I'll tell you who the real leader is in Sales and Marketing: Rob Allison. Narvell just mentioned him. He has come in and taken the worst sales region in the country and made it the best in just about one year's time. And he takes no credit for the turnaround. He pushes the team concept in a sales world and for some weird reason it works. He calls himself the coach and cheers for his team. I wish other sales managers would listen to what he is saying. It obviously works."

Tom looked at Annie with a big grin on his face. "Did you say Rob Allison? As in Robin Allison? About six-foot-one with dark hair? Kind of a big, stocky guy?"

"That's him. Why? How do you know him?" Annie said with just a hint of suspicion in her voice.

"If it is, he worked for us for almost ten years. Quit about three years ago to move back to the northeast somewhere. His wife wanted to be closer to her parents. There were some health issues if I remember correctly. He went to work with a brother-in-law, I think. Man, I'd love to have him back again. He was one of those rare birds. He got the tape measure idea as fast, no ... faster than anyone we've ever hired. Narvell, there's someone you should definitely talk to."

This new revelation had Narvell suddenly thinking about the sales numbers he had seen for Rob's team. As he sat and stared at Tom, he was actually trying to replay those numbers in his head.

"Narvell? You still with us?" Tom asked and waved a hand out at Narvell.

"Oh, sorry. I was just thinking about the Northeast sales numbers. I was trying to recall what all were in those very simple numbers on the board, and even more importantly, in the computer."

"Narvell, speaking of numbers, I was asking about your company metrics. Who decides what to measure? And how many measurements are there?" Tom asked.

"VPs and directors, I guess. Maybe the exec team? I'm not sure. Thinking about the Northeast sales guys though, I'm not sure. Maybe it's the managers in each department. As to the how many .... I'm not completely sure. I do know that it's well over four hundred different things."

"Wait a minute. I don't mean, what does every manager measure to run their team by? I mean, how many metrics are there that are reported up the food chain to measure the success of the company? Is it twenty, thirty, maybe fifty?"

"No sir. It's well over four hundred. There are hundreds and hundreds of metrics on the wall of lame, er ... uh, the metric board, outside the main break room at the plant. I quit counting somewhere around that number."

Now Tom appeared a bit dazed. "Really?" And Annie began to nod yes with Narvell. "Well then, let me ask another question. How many key performance indicators are on that board?"

Narvell thought about this question for quite a while. He looked at Annie for help, but all she could do was shrug her shoulders. Finally, he looked up at Tom and said, "I have no clue what the KPIs are for our company. There is absolutely nothing that causes any of those metrics to stand out as an overall indicator of what our company measures for success at the top level."

Tom stood up from his chair, walked over to the refrigerator, pulled a bottle of root beer out in one hand, then grabbed three beers with his other hand, and came back to the group. "All right. Last question: How flexible of an organization is Burdette? How fast can you respond to customer issues?"

Narvell pounced on this question. "Sir, personally I think we suck at being flexible. Apparently, we have a very rigid set of rules that govern how, when, and how long the engineering team should take for any and all requests. It doesn't seem to matter whether it is a simple costing question, or if it is a major new product project. We respond according to the predetermined schedule. Period. End of discussion. And we still use a flippin' spreadsheet to do costing calculations even though our new ERP system, that has been installed now for months, has a great costing module in it. We keep doing it the old way. Is it because that's the way we've always done it or because of pride of ownership? I don't know. But it sure screams that we don't like change." Narvell finished this last answer with his arms waving and his voice elevated almost to a scream, showing his frustration with his own department.

"Whoa there, Narvell. Calm down. I didn't mean to strike a nerve. But can I give you a bit of advice?" Tom said leaning forward towards Narvell's chair.

"Oops. Sorry, sir. Sure. I can always use good advice."

"First of all, if you don't know why you still use the spreadsheet, don't jump to conclusions. Second, be careful how you speak about it and to others. The way you responded to my question just now would have put many people in your department on the defensive, I suspect. Think, and then speak in thoughtful consideration of those around you. Trust me on this one. I have made that mistake many a time in my career. Thankfully, I have had good mentors and peers around me to keep me from short-circuiting my career. Understand?"

"Yes, sir. I think I do," Narvell said, completely focused on Tom now.

"Good. Now I have one piece of advice for you. Think back about what we just discussed and then go find the answers. Any way you can. Just don't get yourself fired. Okay? Ask any and everyone you know inside the company to help flesh it out. Remember, Narvell, you are searching for the truth, not trying to start a revolution or make enemies. When you're done, if you and Chris want to continue the discussion on your own, great. If you want to talk to me again, I'm more than happy to sit down with you. Oh, and Annie. I guess you can tag along to help keep these two guys in line." Tom finished it off with a very deliberate wink Annie's way and then he laughed.

Annie joined in and then shook her head slowly. "Tom, you can flatter me all you want. But … I am not getting back together with your son." And at that, both Annie and Chris laughed.

***

As soon as Narvell got home that night, he went straight to his room and logged into his computer. Opening his Web browser, he quickly logged into his blog and started typing in the questions Tom had asked him. As he typed each one, he thought through the whole list again, just to make sure he wouldn't forget one.

People and Measurements

Posted on **September 22, 2011**
Reply

The tape measure isn't just about how you measure. It also has to do with the people. Who are the leaders? Not the managers of the company, the leaders! And just as important, how do employees respond to the managers AND these leaders?
A few questions to find answers to:

- What does the story of the tape measure really mean?
- Who are the leaders at M.E. Burdette Co.?
- How do our employees respond to our managers?
- How do our employees respond/interact with our leaders?
    * Try to SEE the leaders!!!
    SIDE BAR – Who is Rob Allison? Call him.
- How many measurements do we have as a company?
- Who decides what to measure?
- What are our Key Performance Indicators (KPIs)?

Take the time to answer these questions. And don't put people on the defensive. You are trying to find answers, not create enemies.

Posted in Blogs from the book | Leave a reply

Chapter 10

The Journey for Answers

September 26

Monday morning came way too soon as far as Narvell was concerned. As he drove to the office, he kept replaying the previous week over and over in his head. The more Narvell thought about the chaos of the previous week, the more he dreaded walking into the Engineering department that morning. When he turned the corner and came through the door into Engineering, Narvell really expected Bill Cooke to be standing there waiting for him. The reality, though, was a pleasant surprise. The hallway was empty.

Sitting down at his desk in the small cubicle, Narvell did something very uncharacteristic. Instead of logging into his computer and checking his e-mail as he had done every morning since he had started to work at M.E. Burdette Co., Narvell pulled a copy of Tom Anselmo's questions from his pocket and began to study them. Narvell thought about how to get each of these questions answered. He wondered how he could ever come up with a complete list of the leaders in their company. Just as he began to fold up the list of questions, his phone rang. He glanced at the display showing the internal extension number and then reached for the phone.

"Hi, Annie. What's up?"

"Hi, Narvell. Do you have time to come over to Marketing? There's someone here you might want to talk to."

"Well, since the entire engineering management staff is in their weekly meeting this morning, I don't see why not. I've got nothing on my plate. I'll be over in a couple of minutes. Who is it anyway?"

"Nope. I'm not saying. Come over and find out. Bye."

Narvell logged into his computer and checked to see if he had any e-mail worth reading, then put his phone on "Do Not Disturb" before he headed out the door. As he walked down the hall and turned into the stairwell to go downstairs, Narvell tried to figure out who it could be that Annie wanted him to meet. Talking quietly to himself, Narvell continued towards Marketing. "Does it have anything to do with this, this … What the heck is this journey, no investigation, uh, adventure. No, that's not right. What have I gotten myself into anyway? Oh man, I'm driving myself crazy now. It's probably just someone else from college. Who else works here? I'm sure there are more than just the two of us."

Narvell was so into personal conversation that he almost walked right by the door to Marketing. When he realized what he was doing, he stopped so abruptly that he nearly tripped over his own feet. Turning quickly and entering the marketing department offices, Narvell scanned the area looking for Annie.

"Narvell. Over here," Narvell heard a voice shout from off to his right. Looking towards the far end of the area, Narvell saw Annie standing in a door with a sign next to it that said *MWR 1*. As he walked through the department, he noticed that the cubicles in this department had very low divider walls. Low enough that not only could you see the entire area from any point in the department, but you could also see everyone sitting in their cubicles. The strangest thing to Narvell, though, was the fact that it was surprisingly quiet.

When he got to the door where Annie was standing, he walked in and found himself face to face with Rob Allison, Northeast Region sales manager. Narvell had not been expecting this and was so suddenly caught off guard that he was speechless. But, as usual, Annie came to his rescue. "Narvell, I believe you and Rob have already met. I hope you don't mind, but Rob was in the office this morning talking to George when I got here. He came by and asked me how things were going, so I may have said a thing or two about what happened last week, and then I might have said a teeny tiny bit about Friday night at Chris' parents."

Narvell could feel his face turning red. But before he could say anything, Rob reached out, shook his hand, and waved him into a chair. "Sit down, Narvell. I believe I told you last week after that rather odd meeting that I liked what you and Jimbo said. I meant it. You two spoke your piece. From where I was sitting, it sounded like the two of you were the ones that broke the meeting open. What you said set the stage for everyone else that spoke up. I also heard about Bill's outburst. When Annie told me that you were trying to figure out the financial problem on your own, I asked her if there was anything I could do to help you. After all, no one else has come to the table with a way to turn the tide. So I guess why I'm here is to ask, what can I do for you?"

Narvell was a bit stunned by the latest twist in his journey to find out why M.E. Burdette Co. was losing money in spite of all the good things that appeared to be going on in the company. "Well, sir, I really don't know where to start. I hadn't expected anyone to stand up and join my somewhat crazy adventure. But …. I really want to talk to you about your metrics on the board outside the break room," Narvell finally managed to say.

"You mean someone really reads that garbage on the wall?" Rob said and then laughed. "Sorry. I hope I didn't just offend you. You aren't responsible for any of the thousand numbers plastered on the wall, are you?"

"No, sir. You mean you aren't impressed with all the information?"

"Not in the least, Narvell. And please, call me Rob. There might be some good data buried in there somewhere. I suppose if our region's metrics are posted, then there are at least three good ones. But for the most part, I would call it overkill. Plain and simple, there is way more data on that wall than anyone can ever digest. I think if you started now, you might get about 20% of the way through it before it all changes again. Okay now, you said you wanted to talk about our metrics. What do you want to know?"

"Why three? I mean Rob, when you look at what every other sales team and every other department posts for metrics, yours seems a bit thin. And yet, the results are amazing. How do you do it?" Narvell said, leaning forward towards Rob.

"First of all, let's talk about the three metrics. That's all we need. After sitting down with our team when I first came on board, that's what we decided on. Those three metrics are kind of like a tape measure. We report out a set of simple numbers that make sense to the team and accurately portray our progress. There's no reason to use thirty seconds when using quarter-inch increments will do. Sorry, I hope that analogy makes sense?"

"So you *are* the Robin Allison who used to work at Housholder Sprockets!" Narvell almost shouted as he jumped from his seat. "Wow. Maybe you can help me."

"Calm down, Narvell. How did you know I used to work for Housholder? And why should that mean I can help you?"

"Oh, uh … sorry, Rob. Mr. Anselmo was wondering if it was you when I explained how good your metrics were and said that there were only three of them. "

"You know Tom and Max?" Now Rob was leaning towards Narvell.

"Tom, yes. I was his son Chris' roommate one year in college. Who's Max?"

"Max Housholder. Tom's father-in-law. The chairman of Housholder Sprockets. He would be Chris' grandfather. Great guys. If Chris is anything like his father and grandfather, you've got a friend for life. Why were you explaining our problems to them?" Rob said in a low and somewhat skeptical voice.

"Well, after the crap that went down last week, I was feeling pretty down. Annie …" Narvell said looking around only to find that Annie had left the room, "took me to meet Chris for dinner at his parents. I thought Annie told you all this?"

"She just said that you two met an old college roommate for dinner. Something about him trying to help you sort through the data you've looked at and find some answers. I had no idea it was at Tom's house. Continue."

"Well anyway, Chris told me the story of the tape measure and sent me out to find mine."

At that statement, Rob started laughing. "Find it yet?" he said between chuckles.

"You've been there, huh?"

"Oh yeah. Took me about a month to get it all figured out. But, once you get it, it becomes a part of you. Where were we?" Rob said, trying to steer the conversation back to the topic. "Okay, back to the metrics. Why should I report out a whole lot of numbers and data that have no real impact on the top or bottom line of the company? The three that we use say it all."

"But Rob, how do you run an entire sales region on just three numbers?"

"I don't, Narvell. I think that is where most people struggle with Max's philosophy. I still measure individual performance, as well as several other things like largest single order, biggest increase from last month for our team members, and the list goes on and on. But does any of that really matter? Ultimately, this is what we get measured on. By using a simple set of team metrics, everybody focuses on the team goals; some people ahead of their own, and others after they've hit the personal ones. It doesn't matter as long as we keep getting better as a team."

"So then how do you set your goals?" Narvell asked as he began to realize this might be the break he was searching for.

"Simple. Better than last year. Better than last quarter. Better than last month."

"What? How does that work?" Narvell suddenly asked, somewhat confused. "Don't you have to have a target number? A hard goal or something?"

"Why? If we're constantly getting better than we were last month, or quarter or even last year, aren't we helping the company reach its goals? And in the end that means that each of our team members are getting better, right?"

That last statement suddenly hit Narvell like a ton of bricks. He paused briefly and thought over the tasks that Tom had asked him to investigate, and then looked at Rob.

"Narvell, you just thought of something, didn't you?"

"I did. Now I think I understand why Tom was asking me about leaders and how employees respond to our leaders and managers. If you aren't leading but just managing your people, you don't get the kind of results that you are talking about, do you?"

"I *don't* think so. If your workforce isn't prepared and willing to join you as participants in the journey, and if there is no ownership in the message you are delivering, it's not going to happen. Did Tom explain all this?" Rob said, halfway expecting Narvell to confirm what he suspected.

"No. He asked me who our leaders are and how our employees react to them. And then he went on to ask about our metrics and KPIs. He asked who decides what to measure. Who does decide that anyway?"

"Depends on who you ask. With my sales team, it was the team. When I got hired, the first thing I did was spend a solid week with my team; meeting and getting to know them, explaining my management philosophy, teaching them what my expectations were. We talked about what we needed to change to be successful. We spent five long days getting to know each other and it has been well worth it. Informal training was all my team needed. And to know they are *their* team. I'm not the *boss*. I'm the mentor and cheerleader. We all have a common goal and it's my job to help all of us reach that goal. Anything I can do to make each team member successful is what I try to do every day. And the team has responded by adopting the same philosophy. We have complete ownership in what we do. Yes, each member still has individual goals and objectives. But the biggest bang for the buck, and biggest payout commission and bonus, is to make sure the team collectively hits its goals. Some people would say that our team has done drunk the Kool-Aid. But I say no, we just understand what the company needs from us and we truly function as a team.

The other sales managers that have asked me about our metrics have all said that they decided on their measurements with our VP, Allyson, when I asked. I can't answer for the three or four other sales managers. I haven't spoken to them about the subject. I *can* tell you that George worked with his entire team, including Annie, in setting their goals. However, from what I have been told, they did not select the metrics as a team. George did that outside of the group and then reviewed them with everyone to get *buy-in*. Ask Annie if she knows who George worked with on the actual metrics."

Narvell thought about what Rob had just told him, then continued. "So what about Accounting? Engineering? Manufacturing? Facilities and the other support functions? Any idea about their metrics? And the biggie I really want to know is … what are our KPIs? I haven't found anything specifically stating the top level metrics on the board or on the server."

Rob looked up just in time to see Bryan Steinman, one of the oldest and longest tenured mechanical engineers in the company, come walking into the room. "Hi, Bryan. What's up?"

"Rob … What's this troublemaker doing over here in Sales & Marketing? Shouldn't you be at your desk costing something out or whatever it is you do, kid?"

Narvell just stared at the newcomer in the room since he had no idea who Bryan was and really didn't know how to respond with the limited amount of knowledge he had about the man. Rob stood up in between Bryan and Narvell and faced Bryan before speaking. "Bryan, I really don't care why *you* are here. But, I do care about the way you just spoke to someone I asked to meet with me this morning. So, if you need something, tell me. Otherwise, I'd like for you to leave."

"Actually I do need something, Rob. One of your team put in for a customization of a standard series of cremation urns that we have been making for years. When I suggested that he sell the existing line to his customer, he said no. His customer wants a few changes. When I said that would take six weeks, he told me he needed them in two and that if I didn't like it, I could talk to you. So here I am. Six weeks, period."

"Not good enough, Bryan. Jack is trying to sell an entire line to the largest funeral home company in the northeast United States. All he's asking for is for you to take the Classic Collection line, reduce the height of each urn by half an inch, taking it out of the middle, and make it available in bronze and pewter. This could be a quarter million dollar account."

"Six weeks, Rob. You know the rules. Our engineering guidelines are not negotiable. You'll have the drawings and spec sheets on November 6th. And if I were you, I'd stay away from this guy. He's trouble. I saw what he did to Bill in the meeting with Fred. He won't last very long here. I can promise you that. Bill doesn't allow people who don't follow the rules to stay on his team." And with that, Bryan walked out.

"Well, you really made an impression on him, Narvell."

"Rob, I don't even know him. I've only seen him a couple of times from across the department and then in the conference room for the last two meetings we had. This sucks. What have I done other than simply ask a few questions and say what was on my mind about the way we do some things?" Narvell suddenly was feeling all of the air leave his body like a balloon with a slow leak. As he began to slump in the chair, Rob sat back down and placed a hand on Narvell's shoulder. "Narvell, do not let Bryan or anyone else, including Bill, get to you. You've done nothing wrong. Understand?"

"Yeah, I guess. So what do I do now?"

"Well, you can start by asking Annie what she knows about Marketing's metrics. Then I would suggest that you talk to Jimbo about who set Engineering's up. Also, if you want, I have an old friend in manufacturing named Ed McIntosh. He's been a shift supervisor for nearly ten years. Go see him and ask about their metrics. Tell him I sent you and said for him to be discreet. He's a good guy and won't go telling everyone that you were snooping around asking questions. When you are done getting those things answered, then call Tom Anselmo and meet with him again. I'd love to see you get this all figured out. Call me if you need anything else, all right? I've got to run. I have another meeting and then a plane to catch. Good luck."

"Thank you, Rob. I appreciate the help."

Both Narvell and Rob walked out of the room together and headed off in opposite directions. Narvell stopped by Annie's cubicle on his way back to Engineering, but she wasn't at her desk. He decided that he'd call her later and continued on down the corridor to the break room. When he got there, Narvell poured himself a cup of coffee and sat down to think about what Rob had told him. He replayed the conversation multiple times to make sure he could remember it all. When he finally looked up at the clock on the wall, he realized he had been in the break room for almost an hour, so he stood up and headed back upstairs to Engineering.

When he got there, Bill was standing in front of his cubicle talking to Jimbo. As he walked up, Bill looked at him and then back at Jimbo. "We'll talk about it later." Bill said to Jimbo and then walked off.

"What's up, Jimbo? And what was that all about?" Narvell asked as he walked up.

"Let's just say that Bill is still bent out of shape about our little meeting, Narvell. And to make it worse, Fred just called him and wants you to come to his office at 1:30 this afternoon. Bill said he didn't get an explanation why, just that he wanted to see you. I think that may have pissed Bill off almost as much as what we both said in the meeting last week. Anyway, I suggest you go to lunch and then go see Fred. Let me know what it's all about, okay?"

"Sure, Jimbo. But can I ask you one question?"

"Shoot."

"Who decided the metrics that Engineering uses to report our successes and failures?"

"Narvell, you've got to be kidding? You're still on this kick. You have got to watch your back. Bill is not a happy camper right now. Please let all of this die down."

"No, Jimbo. I want to know. Do you know or not?"

"Okay. It's your ass. Don't say I didn't warn you. Bill, Bryan, and a guy named Steve Russell who quit about two years ago."

"And how much input did the rest of the department have? Did you have any say in how you measured or when?" Narvell sounded as if he was a police detective interviewing a suspect.

"None. Bill, Bryan, and Steve are also the ones that created our policies and procedures. Not just in relation to the metrics … everything. They established the world we live in today. And while they may be a bit inflexible, you've got to admit that there is very little chaos in Engineering."

"Well, Jimbo, there shouldn't be *any* chaos with as much padding as is built into these schedules. I just listened to Bryan tell Rob Allison that he would have drawings and spec sheets on a very simple change on a five-product funeral line done in six weeks. It will probably take a drafter a couple of hours to make the changes, about the same amount of time for Bryan to copy and update the spec sheets, and since I know that we already have other urns cast in the same metals that Rob asked for, it shouldn't take that long to get quotes back from Purchasing."

"Ouch. You're learning fast, my boy. Now please, keep your mouth shut if you want to survive. Fred … 1:30 … Don't be late." Before Jimbo turned to leave, he flashed a slight grin and nodded at Narvell as if to show his agreement with what Narvell had just said.

Chapter 11

A Career Cut Short

Narvell showed up in Fred Schmidt's outer office a full ten minutes before his scheduled appointment. He had no idea why he was here. He really wasn't even sure if he wanted to be here. But, he decided that listening to Jimbo's advice was probably the smartest thing he could do at the moment. He walked in the door and was met by a cheery voice.

"May I help you?" Pat Jacobs, Fred's administrative assistant, asked looking up from her computer screen.

"I have a 1:30 appointment with Mr. Schmidt. I'm Narvell Mann from Engineering, ma'am," Narvell said nervously.

"Oh yes. Mr. Schmidt is expecting you. But, you're a bit early. He's on the phone. Please sit down. He'll be right with you."

"Thank you," Narvell said politely as he sat in one of the large wingback chairs across the room from Pat's desk and the closed door leading into Fred Schmidt's office.

Narvell sat quietly for only two or three minutes waiting for Fred. However, it seemed like an eternity to the young man as he thought about why he had been summoned to the president and CEO's office on this Monday afternoon. Suddenly, the door opened and out walked Fred Schmidt. Coming across the room to meet Narvell, Fred looked both relaxed and at the same time very focused on his visitor. "Narvell, right?"

"Yes, sir."

"Great. Come on in. We have a few things to talk about." And with that, Fred turned about and headed back into the office.

As Narvell stood and followed him, he glanced at Pat who was once again staring at her computer screen. She looked up briefly and flashed a smile at Narvell as he passed her desk. Entering Fred's office, Narvell was somewhat taken back by the plainness of the room. A large cherry-colored executive desk at one end and a small conference table at the other end. There were five oil paintings on the walls that all appeared to be by the same artist, a few framed certificates of accomplishment, and an award or two along with a couple of diplomas.

"Sit down, Narvell. Let me put my phone on 'Do Not Disturb.' It will just take a second," Fred said as he motioned towards the conference table and then turned back to his desk to set his phone.

"Narvell, you're probably wondering why I asked to see you. Am I correct?"

"Yes, sir," was all Narvell could squeeze out of his mouth, because he was so nervous now.

"I had a conversation this morning about you, and I thought it best to get the facts straight from the horse's mouth, as they say," Fred said sitting down across from Narvell. At that statement, Narvell began to wonder how much trouble he was in, and just what all Bill had said to bring him to this office. But as Narvell thought about it, it all began to make sense. Bill walking off and leaving Jimbo to tell him when he had returned to his cubicle. *And why were they standing in front of my desk anyway?* thought Narvell. But what he heard next came as a big surprise.

"Son, I heard you have been trying to understand why we are struggling financially. It is an absolute pleasure to find an entry-level employee—come to think about it, any employee—that is that interested in the success of the company. Did I hear correctly?"

"Well … yes sir. I thought maybe if I could understand what was going on, maybe I could help the company, and at the same time, I would learn more information about M.E. Burdette that could help me move up in the future. However, based on a few of the meetings I've been in lately, I'm not so sure I'll get the chance to move up."

"Whoa, now. Hold on a second, son. We may be experiencing a little turbulence, but I can assure you that we will still be in business this time next year."

"Oh, no, sir, Mr. Schmidt. I was referring to what Jimbo and I said in the meeting last week. We kind of pissed off, if you will pardon the language … Bill. He apparently is still mad about it."

Fred laughed and then responded to this new statement. "Don't worry about Bill. He's a bit of a blowhard, but he means well. And, he's run a very tight ship in Engineering for many years now. But let's not talk about Bill. I want to discuss what you have been looking for."

"What's that, Mr. Schmidt? I'm not sure I know exactly where you are coming from."

"Right, right. Let me back up a bit. Rob Allison stopped by my office before he headed to the airport and told me I needed to visit with you. Rob's a pretty sharp guy and I value his opinion. He has done one helluva job turning around his sales region. He said you had bumped into him after the meeting last week and then again this morning. Said you were asking about metrics and KPIs, and something about leaders versus managers. Rob thought you might have a set of questions that we should be asking our entire management team. So … I'm asking you … What have you been asking about?"

"Oh!" Narvell exclaimed. This twist in the conversation was not at all what he had expected. Nor was it coming from a direction that he had even considered. "Well sir …"

"Narvell, please call me Fred. It will make it a lot easier for us to talk man to man if you will drop the formalities."

"Yes, sir … er … uh … okay. Without going all the way back to the update meeting I attended earlier this month, I think I can explain my actions and the basis of my questions."

And with that simple introduction, Narvell spent the next forty minutes recounting what had happened to him over the past two-and-a-half weeks. As he told his story, he attempted to try and tell it without emotion, to avoid making it sound like he was out to get anyone in trouble. He ended his tale by explaining the dinner and conversation he had had with Chris and Tom Anselmo, the tale of the tape measure, and the list of questions Tom had asked him to answer. He even added some things he suspected were going on at M.E. Burdette Co. in relation to managers versus leaders, as Tom had explained during their conversation. And as he spoke, he realized that there were some things he had learned in college that now made sense, like preparing the workforce for change, training, and employee involvement in the change from the beginning. When he was finished, Narvell took a deep breath and sat back in his chair, not knowing what to expect from Fred.

"Wow, Narvell. I wish all our employees had your dedication. We wouldn't be in the financial shape we're in today if everyone cared this much. I must admit that as I listened to your explanation about what you've done, I forgot to write down your questions you were going over with Rob this morning. Can you e-mail them to me when you get back to your desk? I think I know how to get some, if not all the questions answered fairly quickly. Would you like some help?"

"You bet. Thank you, Fred. I was beginning to think that maybe I'd made a bad career choice. I feel a lot better about all this. I'll e-mail you my questions when I get back to my desk."

"Super. Narvell, I think you have a very bright future here at M.E. Burdette. I'll get with you after I have a chance to review the questions and get a group together to get our answers."

Narvell took this last statement as the end of the meeting, so he stood to leave. Fred stood with him and extended his right hand to shake. "Thank you again, Narvell. I appreciate you and every employee that has your same dedication. Please remember that my door is always open to you."

With that, Narvell turned and walked out of Fred's office. As he walked past Pat Jacobs' desk, he glanced her way. She was staring right at him this time with a big smile on her face. "Your meeting with Mr. Schmidt went well, I assume?" Pat asked.

"Yes ma'am. Thank you," Narvell said without breaking stride as he walked out into the corridor and back towards Engineering.

***

Sitting at his computer, Narvell quickly opened a new e-mail and looked up Fred Schmidt's e-mail address in the company's global address book. He picked Fred's name from the list in front of him and populated the **To** field, then added a subject into the **Subject** field titled "The questions you requested." Narvell then opened his Web browser, navigated to his blog page, and logged in. He then copied and pasted Tom's questions into the e-mail. He had to renumber the questions since he found a few mistakes he had made in his original blog entry, and he had to remove his personal comments from the middle of the list. Before he sent it, Narvell sat and read it over several times to make sure he wasn't forgetting anything.

As Narvell clicked on the **Send** button, the intercom on his telephone beeped and a voice came over the phone. "Narvell, it's Bill Cooke. Come to my office." And then Narvell heard the phone go dead. So, he minimized the e-mail application on his desktop and walked down the hall to Bill's office. When he arrived, Narvell walked in to find Bill sitting at his desk. "Close the door, Narvell."

I'm in Town
    From: Narvell.Mann
      To: Fred.Schmidt

Add to Contacts

Mr. Schmidt-

Here are the questions we discussed this morning:

1. Who are the leaders at M.E.Burdette Co.?
2. How do our employees respond to our managers?
3. How do our employees respond/interact with our leaders?
4. How many measurements do we have as a company?
5. Who decides what to measure?
6. What are our Key Performance Indicators (KPIs)?

Thank you again for meeting with me.

Narvell T. Mann
Cost Analyst, Engineering
M.E. Burdette Co.

***

"Narvell, calm down. I can't understand you when you're screaming into the phone." Chris had answered his cell phone and had to move it away from his ear Narvell was yelling so loud. "Please Narv, take a deep breath and calm down. Slowly now. What's the matter?"

"That SOB fired me. I go off and help the CEO by telling him what we've been talking about and then Bill fires me!" Narvell was still yelling, but at least now Chris could understand him.

"Okay, Narv. Listen to me. Calm down. Where are you?"

"I'm on my way to Bobby's house. I'm going to pack my bags and leave. I'm going home. I'm sick of this crap."

"Narvell, listen very carefully to me for a minute. Please don't do anything stupid. I'm on my way over. Don't leave until I get there … okay?"

"No, it's not okay," Narvell began to yell again. "I never should have taken this stupid job in the first place."

"Whatever, Narv. Just don't do anything you'll regret later. I'll be there in about 10 minutes," Chris spoke into his cell phone and then began thinking about what his next move should be. "Okay? I'll see you in ten." Pushing the **End** button on his cell phone, Chris looked around his office. "What now?" He quickly sent out an e-mail saying that he would be out of the office for the rest of the afternoon and then headed for the parking lot. On his way out of the building, Chris called Annie and told her what was happening. She told Chris she'd meet him there. But before she could ask any questions, Chris disconnected the phone and jumped into his car and headed towards Narvell and Bobby's house.

***

Chris arrived at Narvell and Bobby's house and as he jumped out of his car and headed up the walk, he noticed that not only was Narvell's car in the driveway but Annie's and Bobby's were in the drive as well. He didn't bother knocking when he bounded up onto the front porch. He let himself in and found all three of his friends sitting in the living room. Bobby was seated in a recliner at the end of the room opposite the television, while Narvell and Annie were sitting on the couch. Narvell was facing straight ahead and appeared to be staring at the wall, while Annie was sitting on the couch facing Narvell with both legs crossed up on the cushions.

"Narvell, listen to me. You have got to tell us what is going on. Sitting here staring at the wall cussing at thin air is not going to solve this problem. Do you hear me?" Annie said in a stern yet obviously concerned voice. "Please …"

Bobby looked up from his seat at Chris and chimed in, attempting to lighten the mood a little: "It's about time you got here. Geez, we've all been here at least three or four minutes. Can I please get us all something to drink?"

"Do what you want, Bobby. Just take this whole thing a bit more seriously, would you?" Chris said in a somewhat seething tone, glaring at Bobby.

"I might if someone would bother to tell me what the hell is going on."

Narvell looked over at Bobby and slowly said, "I got fired today. That's what happened."

"Got it. I can respect the seriousness of this conversation. And yes, I do believe that we all need a drink. Be right back." And with that, Bobby popped up from his chair and headed to the kitchen.

Annie, who had looked over at Chris and Bobby, returned her gaze to Narvell. "Talk. Please. Sitting here like this is not helping any."

As Chris walked over and sat down in the second recliner in the room, Narvell turned his head to first look at Chris and then Annie. After ten very long seconds of staring at her, he finally opened up. Never looking at Chris, just Annie, Narvell started in. "That SOB fired me. All I did was tell Schmidt what I was trying to do and then *he* fires me. I even sent Schmidt a copy of the questions from my blog. Next thing you know, I'm sitting at my desk and Bill calls me in and fires me. He accused me of corporate espionage. Said he saw me passing information at a restaurant last week to someone from another manufacturing company in town. When I asked for details, he said he didn't need to disclose any of that; that since I was still on probation, I was being terminated at will. This is all Chris' fault." Narvell's voice was getting louder as he spoke and each sentence was becoming sharper as the anger began to flow from him.

"Why the hell did I ever talk to you about this?" Narvell asked, turning his head towards Chris. "If I had just kept my mouth shut and gone on with life, I would still be fat, dumb, and happy. I might be worried about whether I'd have a job in another six months or a year, but at least I'd have a job right now. You and that damn tape measure. Why did I ever agree to even see you when I came back to town?" And with that final statement, Narvell looked back at Annie with a sad and defeated look on his face and then hung his head.

Chris took the opportunity when Narvell stopped talking to speak up. "Hang on a second, Narvell. Are you telling us that you got fired for trying to solve the company's financial problems? That doesn't make sense."

"Yeah, well maybe it was that stupid story of yours," Narvell said looking up at Chris. "All I know is I did what I thought was right and then Bill lowers the boom on me. This sucks."

Chris exchanged a glance with Annie that seemed to confirm his confusion over the events of the day, then looked back at Narvell. "Can you please tell us exactly what happened? This doesn't exactly make sense."

"How many times do I have to repeat all of this? Fred Schmidt called me into his office this afternoon and wanted to talk to me about what I was doing. He said that Rob Allison had stopped by and suggested that he hear what I was doing. So, I spent an hour or so in his office explaining what I was trying to do. I told him the story of the tape measure. I told him about you and your father, Chris, and how you all had discussed how Housholder Sprockets operates. I told him that I thought that we had a lot of managers trying to do things right, but not many leaders doing the right things. I kinda figured all that out after talking to your dad the other night and then visiting with Rob and Annie.

"Hell, I even talked about the need for change and how we need to train our employees and get them involved in the change. I thought I was doing something good by telling Schmidt all that stuff. Look where it got me. Why did I ever open my mouth? I should have listened to Jimbo and just played dumb."

Just as Narvell finished this last statement, Bobby came walking back into the room with a beer for each of them. "I thought you could probably use something a bit stronger than this. But, it turns out I used all the tequila for margaritas last week and haven't made it back to the liquor store yet. I just want you three to know that I was listening from the kitchen and I think all three of you are missing what's happening here."

"Oh, and you have it all figured out, huh? Okay, big Bobby, tell us. What is this all about?" Narvell said rather sarcastically.

"It's that Bill fella—your boss. He fired you because you're about to find out how he's been stealing millions of dollars from the company. He saw a perfect opportunity since you are still a probationary employee, so he took it. That's probably better than him running you over in the parking lot and claiming it was an accident."

Chris chuckled at Bobby's last remark and started to join in on the theory when Annie caught his eye with an ice-cold look that quickly stopped him before he said anything. Then Annie looked over at Bobby. "Bobby, you are so full of it. And I suppose that Bill didn't even know that Narv had met with Fred? I find your theory a bit hard to believe. How is an engineering director going to steal that much money from a company?"

"I didn't say I had it all worked out. I just …"

Before Bobby could finish his sentence, Narvell's phone rang. He glanced down at the phone and then answered it. "Hello …"

Chapter 12

A Game Changer

Narvell pushed the **End** button on his cell phone and sat staring straight ahead. Everyone else in the room was looking at Narvell expecting him to say something, yet he just stared at the wall on the far side of the living room. The phone call had lasted slightly more than three minutes, but seemed like an eternity to both Annie and Chris as they listened to Narvell's side of the conversation trying to figure out who was on the phone. There weren't many clues from what Narvell had said to the caller, mainly "No, sir" and "Yes, sir." But his body language betrayed his voice. The expression on Narvell's face had gone from confusion to alarm, sudden realization, and then to a look of absolute calm and satisfaction. He had ended the call by saying, "Yes, sir. Thank you. I will." Then he sat quietly staring at the wall.

Finally, Annie could take it no more. "Narvell. Speak. What the heck was that call all about? Who was it?"

Narvell slowly turned his head towards Annie and spoke. "It was Fred Schmidt. He called to say he had heard that Bill had fired me. He called to say that he wasn't going to let that happen." And with that, a very big grin broke across Narvell's face. "He said he would take care of it in the morning. Then he said I should take tomorrow off, so he could ask some questions around the office and follow up on one issue. He wants to meet with me at the Alumni House on campus for breakfast Wednesday morning. He wants me to work directly for him."

And with that, Narvell started laughing. Annie jumped up from where she was sitting and nearly knocked the couch over as she jumped on top of Narvell, hugging him and laughing right along with him. Chris and Bobby sat and watched the spectacle in front of them; Bobby with a bit of confusion and wild speculation going through his mind, and Chris feeling completely satisfied.

When the laughter had finally subsided, Bobby looked at Narvell with Annie lying on top of him. "Looks like your new boss is about to catch your old boss with his hand in the cookie jar. Told ya so."

"Bobby, knock it off. I still don't think anyone has stolen millions of dollars from the company. I think you are way off on this whole thing. But it does make me feel better to know that someone at the top thinks I'm on to something," Narvell said, moving Annie into a sitting position and then sitting up next to her.

"Okay. Don't believe me. But this does call for a celebration. Let's go get some pizza or something to celebrate your new position," Bobby replied, standing up. "Who's with me?"

A resounding chorus of "Me!" came from the other three, who then stood up and headed for the door, following Bobby.

***

When the foursome returned from a dinner of pizza and beer at Altruda's restaurant, which was located on the edge of campus, Chris stopped his car in front of Bobby and Narvell's house. Bobby opened the front passenger door and nearly fell out of the car. Stumbling across the lawn, he managed to make his way to the front porch and unlocked the door before either Annie or Narvell could get out of the car. Chris shook his head at the sight and laughed.

Narvell pulled himself up out of the seat and held the door open for Annie, then leaned back into the open door. "Chris … thanks for the support, man. I really do appreciate it. I was way off base earlier today. You didn't deserve that. I'm sorry. I'll call you Wednesday after I meet with Mr. Schmidt."

"Don't worry about it, Narv. I understand. I probably would have done the same. Get a good night's sleep and take it easy tomorrow. You never know what will come of this new job. You may still want to kill me after Schmidt tells you what he wants you to do," Chris replied with a chuckle.

Narvell stood back up and closed the car door. He stood and watched as Chris pulled away before he turned back to Annie. To his surprise, she was right in front of him, really closer to wearing his shirt, actually, when he turned around. Annie reached out and hugged Narvell around the neck and whispered in his ear. "I am so glad this is getting fixed. Narv, I just want you to know that I am proud of you for sticking with this." She continued to hug Narvell and in response, he wrapped his arms around her and returned the hug.

After thirty or forty seconds, Annie suddenly leaned back, kissed Narvell on the cheek and pulled away. Before returning to her usual high-energy self, Annie stared deep into Narvell's eyes, and then as if turning on a switch, she was full speed once more. "Gotta run, Narvie. I've got two meetings in the morning that I still need to do some research on. Call me after work tomorrow, okay?" And before he could answer, Annie was halfway across the yard to her car parked in the driveway. Opening the car door, she waved at him before disappearing into the driver's seat.

Narvell watched as Annie backed out of the drive and into the street. His eyes didn't leave her car until it was only a shadow moving down the darkened street. Narvell thought through the last few minutes and realized that maybe there was something between the two of them. With a smile on his face, he walked up the sidewalk and into the house. Bobby was sitting there waiting. "Man … she's got it bad for you!"

"You really think so, Bobby?" Narvell said with the smile still on his face.

"Yes. And you got it bad for her, too. So when you gonna do something about it, *Narvie*?" When Bobby said Narvie his voice went up several octaves in a half-hearted attempt to impersonate Annie.

"It just seems a little weird to start dating Chris' ex while I'm hanging around with him. Especially since he has been helping me with this whole thing."

"Dude … if Chris had a problem, he would have already said something. Trust me. He knows what's going on. I suspect everyone around you does."

Bobby's last comment hit Narvell in a strange way. Not the part about Chris, but about everyone knowing. He couldn't quite put his finger on it, but he felt strange as soon as Bobby said it. He stood there trying to figure it out, but to no avail. So, he told Bobby good-night and walked to his bedroom.

***

Tuesday came and went without any excitement for Narvell. By the end of the day, he felt as though maybe things would return to normal. Around six o'clock he tried calling Annie but didn't get an answer. He left her a voice-mail and as he hung up, he wondered where she might be and what she was doing at this very moment.

When Annie hadn't called him back by eight, Narvell tried calling her again. Still no answer. About ten minutes later, he got a text message from her. "Stuck in planning session. Can't talk now. Call u later." Later never came. Narvell finally gave up on talking to Annie and went to bed a little after midnight.

Waking up in the morning, Narvell found a text message on his phone from Annie. All it said was, "Sorry. Talk later." This made him feel a bit better as he prepared for his breakfast meeting with Fred Schmidt. Narvell made sure that he left in plenty of time to get to the Alumni House on campus. The Alumni House was a popular meeting place for business leaders in town who wanted to meet off-premises in private. Breakfast, lunch, and dinner were served in rooms accommodating anywhere from two to twenty people. Many of the larger businesses in town made large donations to the university alumni association to ensure that this quaint and safe place to conduct business would not fall victim to any budget cuts.

Walking in the front door of the Alumni House, Narvell asked the young lady at the front desk where he could find Fred Schmidt. She directed him to a small room at the back of the first floor just off the main hallway. Walking in, Narvell was shocked by who he saw sitting at the table with Fred Schmidt.

Fred stood when he saw Narvell. "Narvell, glad you could make it. I believe you know these two gentlemen," Fred said as he gestured towards Tom and Chris Anselmo sitting to Fred's left. "And this is Max Housholder, Chairman and CEO of Housholder Sprockets."

Even though Narvell was still stunned by the presence of the Anselmos, he managed to reach out and shake Max Housholder's hand. "Nice to meet you, Narvell. I've been hearing quite a bit about you the last few days."

"Nice to meet you, too, sir," Narvell said. He then looked at Chris as if to say, "What is going on?" Chris just looked back at him and smiled.

"Sit down, Narvell," Fred continued. "Breakfast will be served shortly. But before we get to the food, I want to talk about a couple of things first."

Narvell sat down at the remaining seat at the table and slowly looked at all three of the others. "Okay. Let's talk. About what, sir?"

"Well … oh, and would you please stop calling me 'sir'? I know it's the polite thing to do, but I really want to get past that. We need help as a company. You are interested in finding the answers and that's more than I've gotten from just about every one of the exec team at this point. So, first let me fill you in on why I asked Max, Tom, and Chris to join us.

"A couple of hours after you left my office, I realized that I hadn't asked you how you thought we could fix the problem. So I called your extension and voice-mail answered with our standard "*he doesn't work here anymore*" message. I immediately called Bill and asked what was going on. He said you had gotten belligerent with him when he confronted you about corporate spying—his words not mine—and that you cussed him out and stormed out of his office. He said since you were still on probation there was only one thing he could do.

"Not five minutes after I hung up from Bill, Jimbo came walking into my office. He didn't knock or even bother to stop and ask Pat if I was in, so I knew from the look on his face that something was wrong. Jimbo came clean and told me about Bill's antics toward both of you over the past few weeks. Instead of calling Bill in to explain himself, I called Rob and had him tell me everything he knew about you. Narvell, let me tell you something. You haven't been with our company very long, but you have really impressed some of our best people.

"This whole incident has me questioning the entire management team. That's why I called Tom. After hearing from Rob, I thought I needed some outside input and I've heard what Tom and Max do in the community. They were gracious enough to meet with us this morning and suggested that Chris come along."

At that point, Max raised a hand slightly as if commanding Fred to stop talking. It worked, and Max then addressed Narvell. "Son, Fred asked us for some direction in finding out what the issues are at Burdette. I told him we would come and discuss the problems, but from what I've heard, he has a really good hand in you. So you need to tell him what needs to be done."

"But Mr. Housholder …," Narvell started to protest.

"No buts. We all need to see if you've learned anything. *And,* we need to see if my grandson has been listening to anything his father and grandfather have been saying for the past, oh … say, twenty-plus years. Please state the problem for us and then tell us what you think is missing."

"Yes, sir." Narvell replied and then took a deep breath.

"I've been giving this a lot of thought. Ever since that first meeting I went to, I've wondered what was missing; what was wrong. I tried looking at our company metrics on the network but got nowhere. The only measurements on the server were from Rob Allison."

"Well, Narvell, all our metrics are displayed on the employee information boards, sometimes referred to as the metric boards or data walls outside the break rooms. Didn't you look there?" Fred asked, trying to be helpful.

"Yes, sir, er, I mean Fred, I did. I looked at the board outside the main break room and quit looking after I'd tried to interpret and memorize somewhere north of a hundred different measurements for just two departments. That's part of the problem. Originally, I thought we did a great job collecting all of that information. Then, after trying to wade through it multiple times, I came to the conclusion that I was lost in it. I had no idea what it meant. Then, after visiting with Chris and seeing Rob Allison's metrics, and I did find them on the server, by the way, I think I figured out the problem. Our metrics have no purpose. Wait, that's not fair. I should say they have no purpose beyond measuring every little thing that happens everywhere in the company. Fred, I don't want to be too bold, but can you answer me a question?" Narvell was looking straight at the CEO now and was getting very comfortable in the conversation.

"Sure, son. Go ahead."

"All right. What are M.E. Burdette Company's key performance indicators?"

"Now we're getting somewhere, Narvell. I like that. Our KPIs are very straightforward. We have six of them. One, we will grow the top line of the company by 10% each year. Two, we will increase the bottom line by 10% each year. Three, we will own a 40% market share in five years. Four, we will be debt free by the end of the decade. Five, we will be the industrial vessel manufacturer of choice in the defense industry within five years. And six, we will introduce twelve new, not redesigned but truly new, products to the market each year. The executive team worked for nearly two months setting these goals, and I'd have to say that they have given us the clearest vision that we've had as a company since I have been here," Fred said directly to Narvell, and then he turned as if to make sure that the other three men in the room understood his comments.

What Narvell said next took Fred by surprise, and caused Max, Tom, and Chris to all smile. "Fred, I don't want to appear argumentative or insubordinate, but, sir, I don't believe those are KPIs at all."

"What?!? What do you mean?" Fred responded, as he looked at the three other men with grins on their faces.

"You just stated six very honorable goals. But they are not KPIs. They are goals. How do we measure the first goal? The one about the top line."

"That's easy, Narvell. The board reviews the P&L with the exec team every quarter."

"What about the second one? The bottom line." Narvell was really beginning to feel good about this as he watched the expressions on Max, Tom, and Chris' faces brighten a bit more with each statement and question.

"Same as the first. The board reviews it each quarter with the exec team," Fred said starting to sound a little bit irritated.

"Well then, how does Sam out in the fabrication department know how we are doing in regards to this metric? And, oh by the way, what happens when we reach that 10% goal? Do we stop trying? I believe that key performance indicators are just that, indicators. They are a measuring tool, not a goal. And more importantly, any and all metrics we use to show how good, or bad, we are doing must be seen and understood by all employees. Am I right, Mr. Anselmo?" Narvell glanced over at Tom, looking for the affirmation of his idea.

Max spoke first. "Narvell, I think you have this thing nailed. Fred, don't take this the wrong way because goals are very important. But at the same time, showing success, or failure, is actually independent of the goal. One of the major problems with goals in many companies is the tendency to coast once a goal is reached. This is especially true if bonuses are dependent on reaching the goal, and you max out the bonus when the goal is reached. Why get any better if you aren't going to be rewarded any further. Why not just wait for next year to add more to the bonus category?'

Max let Fred chew on his last statement for a few seconds before looking back at Narvell. "Continue, Narvell."

"Yes, sir. As I was saying, all of our employees need to understand what each metric being used as a KPI is. Not just what it is, but what it does and how they affect it. It starts at the top with you, sir. You set the stage. With the management team, you must determine what our KPIs are and then drive them down to the very bottom of the company. It's kind of like using a tape measure to build a house." And at that very moment, Narvell realized that he did indeed now understand what was missing at M.E. Burdette Co. They didn't have a tape measure.

Fred looked at Narvell confused, but when he looked around and saw Chris and Tom chuckling softly and then saw the huge smile on Max's face, he quickly came to the conclusion that this young man named Narvell T. Mann was something special. Interrupting Narvell, Fred asked the question that everyone else in the room expected. "Okay, I think I just got lost. How is measuring the success of our company like using a tape measure to build a house?"

"It's really simple, sir. You are the guy at the top, kind of like the homeowner. What are you interested in? Does the house look good? Are the carpenters building it according to plan? Are they using the right number of studs in the walls, spaced correctly? How do you know? You grab a tape measure when you go by to see their work and check to see if the studs are on 16-inch centers. How do you know if it's correct, very quickly? Easy. Every 16 inches on your tape is marked with a red number, so you know where the studs should be. How do you know they are building it the right size? You measure from one end to the other, generally looking at the number of feet on the tape, right?

"Now, that's you at the top. Let's go down one level. How do your top-level managers know they are successful? Well, they can look at the KPIs you set at the top, but they still need to know if they are succeeding. They have to measure something that says they are doing things right. *And*, whatever they measure must feed your KPIs. It's like they are looking at the inch marks on that tape measure."

Fred started to nod his head as if he was beginning to understand where this was going. Just to make sure, Max spoke up again. "Just because your division heads are using a set of metrics to measure their success and feed the KPIs does not mean that is all they measure. They will continue to measure all kinds of things to ensure that their teams are heading in the right direction. But they only need to report out those few things that tie into the KPIs. Think about it this way. Does every carpenter tell the general contractor every single measurement they take all day long? No. They only report the important stuff. Same thing in business. But, I've interrupted Narvell again. Go on, son. You're doing fine."

"Fred, the point is the farther down the chain we go, the smaller the metric. From foot to inch to half-inch to quarter-inch, eighth-inch, and so on. The trick is that the farther down you go, the more danger there is that the employees won't know what they're measuring and they won't understand how it, or even how they affect the KPIs at the top. That's why you have to keep it simple. And you must prepare the workforce.

"It doesn't take hundreds of metrics to show success. Actually, if you put too much up on the board, you lose most employees. I bet if you ask fifty of our employees at random what metrics are on the board and what they mean, less than five will be able to name more than two or three things on the board. I tried studying the Big Board for days and the only ones that stuck were Rob's. And why? Because they were simple and made sense.

"Mr. Housholder, Mr. Anselmo, I may need some help on this one, but it seems to me that we really only need three to five KPIs for the overall company. And, we probably only need about the same number of metrics at each level of the company as we go down. Maybe three to five in each department, and then when we get to the production floor the same? And would all those work center metrics be the same and roll up into a cumulative number or would they be different?'

Tom could barely contain himself. "Narvell, you are dead on target here. Fred, if you don't want this kid, I want him on my team. There should be a small, three to five is best, set of metrics that feed up and into the overall KPIs. They may be cumulative if all team or work center metrics are identical, or they could be different at the team or work centers and then feed into a cumulative set.

"And yes, Narvell is also right that the employees must understand. They must get it. They must have ownership in it. Not just in reporting the numbers, they must have a hand in deciding what the metrics are. To be successful, you have got to prepare the workforce. Train them and help them understand that they are a part of the process, part of the answer, and part of your success. Max taught me early on that if an employee does not accept their role in the process, they must change or be changed. You have got to prepare your employees for the change that needs to occur. I suspect that Rob Allison has done that with his team. He was very good at teaching his staff when he worked for us. I'd get him involved in this fairly quickly if you're serious about finding a solution."

Fred looked around the table and saw the passion in Max, Tom, and Chris' eyes. But what impressed him most was seeing that same passion and excitement in Narvell's eyes. "I admit I don't quite understand some of the more subtle details of what you are saying, but I know how successful you have been for more than fifty years, Max. I am committing to each of you in this room that M.E. Burdette Co. will change for the better. We have to, or we may not be around this time next year. Max, Tom … We talked earlier about a way to jump-start this. I'm game, if you are? I want to put this plan in place and now.

"Narvell, I have a meeting back at the plant in about twenty minutes, so I'm going to have to leave. But, I want you to stay and talk to these gentlemen about how we are going to implement change. You have until next Wednesday to have a game plan for me. I'm meeting with the exec team Monday and Tuesday to discuss our problems and lack of solutions. I doubt I'll get much more than the same old rhetoric, so you better be ready to roll come Wednesday morning. I'll talk to you later to make sure you don't have any questions."

With that, Fred stood and walked out of the Alumni House.

Chapter 13

Creating the Plan

September 28

"Are you serious?" Narvell asked, staring at Chris in disbelief.

"Serious as a heart attack, Narv."

"How? ... What? ... I mean how is that possible, Chris?"

"Easy. Fred called my dad yesterday and discussed what all had happened. The conversation started with Fred trying to validate your discussion with him in his office. And then it turned into my dad and granddad offering to help. What is good for one employer in town is good for the whole community. It's part of what we do; who we are as a company. So Narvell, whether you like it or not, you are now working with me. Or should I say, I'm working with you." Chris ended his explanation with a big grin on his face.

Narvell looked over at Tom Anselmo and Max Housholder as if he was asking for confirmation without saying a word. Max smiled and nodded in affirmation. Then, both Max and Tom stood up. "Narvell, Fred agreed with me that you and Chris should work on your plan at our offices. We've reserved the room here today until 5:00 p.m., so you both are free to stay here and work. Tomorrow, you'll need to come to our HR office first thing so we can get you an ID badge to get you in and out of the building. I've already arranged for a conference room for you all to work out of. See you tomorrow."

And then Tom and Max walked out.

Chris reached into his backpack next to his chair. He pulled out his laptop computer and a pad of paper. After opening the laptop and turning it on, he looked up at Narvell. "Okay boss, I'm all yours. Tell me what to do."

Heading for the door, Narvell looked back over his shoulder at Chris and replied, "I've got to get my computer out of the car. Log into the blog so we have that piece available to us, and when I get back in with my stuff, we can start talking shop. Be back in a flash."

Narvell nearly ran out to the parking lot to grab his bag. When he got back into the room they had at the Alumni House, he was out of breath. He pulled out his laptop and fired it up. Grabbing a notebook and a pen from the bag, Narvell sat down and stared at Chris.

"Now what?"

"You tell me, Narvell. I'm here to help you remember. Well, that's not completely true. Dad told me on the way over this morning that this was my chance to prove that I have what it takes to join the Housholder team. Since I've never worked anywhere else, this is my opportunity to show dad and granddad that I have enough life experience to run the company some day. Let's go back over the blog and what all you talked about with Fred, and then we can start putting an outline together."

"Sounds like a plan," Narvell answered as he logged into the blog.

***

Narvell and Chris had called Annie midafternoon and offered to buy her dinner. After getting off the phone with them, it dawned on her that something wasn't quite right. After all, why would the two of them be together in the middle of the day? But with an offer for a free meal and plenty of work still in front of her at the office, Annie quickly forgot about what she thought was an odd situation as she plunged back into her work.

When she finally left the office shortly after 5:30 p.m., Annie headed straight for the Aspen Lounge. Not the quietest place in town when it got heated up around 10:00, but for dinner and drinks, it was the place to be for young professionals in this college town; a little too pricey for most college students, but it made for a nice networking location for working singles.

When Annie walked in the door, she saw Narvell and Chris waving at her from a booth across the lounge. They were sitting in the back away from most of the crowd. There were three young, early twenties, females in a booth in the opposite corner, but other than the occasional visitor to that table, everyone else seemed to be staying in the bar area.

As Annie walked up to where Narvell and Chris were sitting, she remembered her curiosity about the phone call earlier in the day. "Okay, boys, what's up? Why were you two together this afternoon?" she asked as she sat down in the booth next to Narvell.

As if ignoring her question, Chris looked at Narvell. "Pay up, Mann. I told you."

Without saying a word, Narvell reached into his back pocket and pulled out his wallet. Opening it up, he pulled out a five-dollar bill and handed it to Chris. And then he smiled.

"What was that for?" Annie asked. "Wait. Answer the first question. *Then* tell me what that was all about," she said looking directly at Narvell.

"Chris and I are now coworkers," Narvell said in his best deadpan voice.

"What? Come on Narvell. Now I'm really confused. You guys quit screwing around with me and tell me what's going on."

"No, really we are," Narvell answered with a grin coming over his face. "Let me explain."

After Narvell had recounted their day for Annie, he waved at the waitress as she was walking back towards the kitchen from the booth in the opposite corner. When she came over to their table, Narvell told her they were ready to order.

Annie looked as if she was even more confused before saying, "But I haven't even seen a menu yet."

"That's okay. Chris already told her what we were eating. She's just going to put the order in now. Don't worry, you'll like it. I promise," Narvell said, hoping that Annie wouldn't bring up the bet Chris and he had made before she came in the restaurant.

"We both feel like we owe you dinner since you stuck with me as I acted like a fool trying to figure this financial thing out at work. *And*, we've made you suffer through being around both of us together at the same time more than you probably wanted to. So… after discussing and debating about what to do, Chris lost the argument and graciously agreed to buy tonight," Narvell looked at Chris to make sure he wasn't backing out of the deal.

Chris nodded to confirm the agreement, then chimed in saying, "Think about this Bean. We work together. Bet you never saw that coming, did you? Narvell and I have exactly six days to create a plan for Fred Schmidt to use to try and turn your, er, I mean our… That's kinda fun to say isn't it? … turn our company around."

"All right Chris, chill." Narvell interrupted. "After we develop this plan and get it implemented, you go back to Housholder. And whether you want to disclose it or not, I will. You are still being paid by *your* company, not ours. And maybe more importantly to your silly story, we are working from an office at your place, remember?"

They all laughed at the absurdity of it all. Then the dinner conversation shifted to other things and they avoided work issues completely. The threesome talked about what their college friends were doing now and tried to figure out where some, who had seemingly disappeared, might now be, working or otherwise. They discussed vacations taken and vacations dreamed of.

The conversation was briefly interrupted when the waitress brought out their meal; Cedar-Plank Salmon for Annie, Red Snapper for Narvell, and Horseradish-Crusted Ahi Tuna for Chris. When they had finished dinner, Chris looked at his watch and then at the two people in the booth across from him. "I hope you don't think it rude of me, but I'm going home. I got up at 4:30 this morning to talk to dad before we came to breakfast, and I'm beat. Narvell, I'll meet you in the HR office at 8:00 a.m. 'Night. guys."

After Chris left, Narvell and Annie sat in the booth and talked as they sipped on their glasses of wine. When the waitress walked up to the table and set down the check, both of them started laughing at the same time. Annie looked at the check and then at Narvell, "Did he do it to you again? How many times over the past three or four years has he burned you on dinner?"

"No clue. That's okay though. I get to sit here in the back of the Aspen Lounge with you and just talk." And with that simple statement, Narvell smiled at Annie. And Annie smiled back, just as Narvell had hoped she would.

What he didn't expect is what happened next. Annie slid over in the booth closer to Narvell and leaned her head on his shoulder. She didn't say a word; she just let her head rest there for what seemed to Narvell like an eternity. And yet, when she lifted it back up and spoke, it seemed as if it had just been a fleeting moment in time. "Narv, thank you."

"For what?"

"For not freaking out about me and Chris. And for being you. Thank you." And then she leaned over and kissed Narvell T. Mann.

***

The next four days went by in a flash, or so it seemed to both Narvell and Chris. They worked on their plan with incredible focus until well after 8:00 p.m. both Thursday and Friday. They met at Chris' house Saturday afternoon and again Sunday afternoon creating much of what they planned on presenting to Fred Schmidt. By Sunday evening they decided that this plan might actually work.

"Narvell, we've got a pretty good start here. But, I'm still not sure how we actually get it rolled out. From the discussion we had Wednesday morning,

I think Fred is expecting us to come loaded for bear. He made a comment to dad on the phone Tuesday that he wanted to give the management team one more chance to come up with answers. That's the reason for the next two days I suppose. He went on to say though that he really didn't expect anything to change. So, the big question here is… If the CEO can't get his team to change, how do we?"

"Look Chris, I don't know either, but we've gotta try something. I just keep thinking back to my organizational behavior class in school and about some of the conversation that I had with Rob Allison. I think we start small. We use Rob as an example and look for one or two other teams or departments that want to play. If Fred can't get the managers to change, maybe they can get each other to change," Narvell replied and then began to give the idea some more thought.

"And I suppose we could always go back to that quote attributed to Jack Welch from General Electric. What did he supposedly say? 'We'll change the people, or change the people.' Maybe that is Fred's fallback position? If someone doesn't want to change, then they get changed. What do you think about that?"

"Nope. We can't go there. At least not say that. We probably want to have that discussion with Fred. But, no ultimatums. There's not a faster way to shut people down than to threaten them. You learned that in school too, didn't you? I mean even I was paying attention that day," Chris said with a laugh.

"Tell you what, Narv. Let's call it a night. We've still got two days before we meet with Fred. I think we can probably finish this up tomorrow and then review it one more time Tuesday. By the way… how'd it go with Annie after I left the other night? I completely forgot to ask you."

"Yeah? And I guess I completely forgot to tell you that you owe me $93.20 for the dinner you were going to pay for, you dog!" Narvell said laughing about it.

"Well? Are you going to answer the question? How did it go? And here's the money for dinner," said Chris as he pulled his wallet out and fumbled around for five twenties amidst all the scraps of paper and receipts falling out of the overstuffed and very worn out old brown leather wallet.

"It was… well… good. No… better than good. When I walked her to her car, she told me that she wasn't going to call me, and that I couldn't call her…"

Chris interrupted. "That doesn't sound very good to me!"

"Let me finish. She doesn't want us to talk until this plan of ours is done. She said she was working on some big marketing deal anyway, and that I'd just be a distraction. But, it's killing me. I want to call her so bad!"

"Focus, dude. Focus. Only a couple more days and then you can see where this big romance is going. Until then, let's not get distracted, okay?"

***

Monday came and went, without too much more progress being made on the M.E. Burdette turn-around plan Narvell and Chris were creating. By day's end, both of the young men were frustrated and they were beginning to feel as if maybe they had bitten off more than they could handle. A phone call to Chris' grandfather put an end to the day very quickly. Max told them to quit trying so hard to create some grand plan and just focus on what they knew was the right thing to do. He told them to turn off their computers and go find a beer. Tomorrow was another day, and they could review and adjust their thoughts in the morning. However, neither felt much like going out on the town, or even sitting on a porch drinking a beer together, so they went their separate ways hoping Tuesday would be better.

Tuesday morning came too early for Narvell. He had spent a restless night dozing off and being awakened by dreams, some that were related to what they were working on and some about Annie. When he came walking into the conference room at Housholder Sprockets that morning, he saw Chris on the phone, not speaking, just listening and then writing feverishly on a legal pad. When he finally hung up the phone, Narvell started up a conversation.

"Before you tell me what that was about, I've got to tell you about my weird dream last night. Actually, I had quite a few. But this one really stuck in my head this morning. I dreamed that Fred had the entire management team in a room… not much of a stretch there, eh? Anyway, in the middle of a speech he was making, one of the people there got up and cussed him out and then walked out. He was screaming about Fred not trusting the team, and then he walked out of the room. Before anything else happened, I woke up. I wonder what is going on at Fred's meeting. Have you thought about it any, Chris?"

"Uh, yeah. But want to hear something even weirder than your dream?" Chris asked but didn't wait for an answer before continuing. "That was Pat Jacobs from Fred's office. You know her?"

"Yes. We've met. Why?"

"She said she was calling for Fred. He wanted us to know that things had gotten a little chaotic at the meeting yesterday. He wants to speed this whole thing up a bit. Pat said we needed to e-mail our slide presentation to Fred by 6:00 p.m. today, so he could review it tonight. We are meeting him here at 7:30 in the morning. He wants to go over it with us and my dad ASAP. How close are we to finishing this thing?"

"I think it's as good as it's going to get. I really like what your granddad said. I went home and thought about it some last night and then put it out of my mind. At least until I started dreaming. I think we lay out the slide show as we have it and then adjust it with Fred and your dad's input. Tell you what, you upload the info into the blog so we have a copy of it there, and I'll review it one last time. We can always go into the blog and edit if I find anything," Narvell said turning on his laptop and opening the presentation file. He then very slowly and carefully began to review the presentation.

***

Fred Schmidt had called the entire top two levels of his management team together for two days to discuss the financial crisis that was nowhere near being resolved. While he had stated very clearly at the kick off of this two-day affair that this was all about finding solutions to put the company back on solid ground, deep down he knew that this would be a repeat of what he had already been through with the executive team.

Monday had indeed gotten a bit chaotic as various managers vocally, and in several instances very aggressively, accused others in the room of being the source of the company's problems. Fred had been forced to break for lunch earlier than planned just to let a few in the room cool off. When they returned in the afternoon, several of the more vocal members of the team in the morning session clammed up. When Fred ended the meeting for the day, he instructed his team to go home and think about the company as a whole. He asked that they come back Tuesday morning thinking holistically about the problem facing M.E. Burdette Co.

And now it appeared as though Tuesday wouldn't be any better than the day before. When Fred walked into the room, he immediately felt the tension in the air. As he looked around, he realized that something was vastly different from Monday. All of the long-time employees were sitting on one side of the room, while the newer members of the management team were seated on the opposite side. Quite different than yesterday, Fred thought as he pictured the scene from Monday, everyone seated in groups by department.

"All right, everyone. Yesterday we laid it all on the table and I know it got a bit hot at times, but we've got to get past this. We need to identify the root cause of our problems and find solutions that will move us forward. I thought we would start today by breaking into small groups and brainstorming. How about if we just split the room down the middle like it's divided now, and then we can split it across this way to form four groups? Any objections?" Fred asked looking around the room for any reaction at all. What happened next took many people in the room by surprise.

Russell Myers, one of the longest tenured sales managers in the company, stood up and began to speak, lecture really. "Fred, I believe that many of us did go home last night and chew on this thing… a lot. I actually made a few phone calls and discussed it with some other managers that are in this room. We are all in agreement on what we know to be the problem. This company hasn't been the same since we started hiring more and more outsiders in as managers.

"These younger people just don't get the culture and way of doing business that has defined M.E. Burdette all these years. We've got to go back to the way we did it for years. We have to grow our managers up inside the company, so that they understand what it is we really do and how we really function. I mean look at how we came in this morning. All of us with real experience in this company are on this side of the room, while the problem sits over there."

Before Russell could get another word out, Fred interrupted him. "Russell, that's enough. What you're saying is just not true and I won't tolerate it. Now, sit down and listen…"

"No Fred… I won't. I'm tired of getting pushed around by these young punks who think they know everything. We need to go back to the way we did it before you were named CEO!" Russell proclaimed defiantly.

Remaining as calm as possible, Fred responded, "Russell, if that were true your sales region would be one of the top teams in the country, wouldn't it? Yet, it's not. You haven't changed your management style one bit since I've been here. And the last time I checked, which was last Friday by the way, your team was next to last in revenue. You have more customers in your market than any other team and you continue to spiral down. So, don't give me any crap about the good old ways of doing business. It's a different world and it requires new and different ways to succeed. So sit down and get with it!"

"I don't have to put up with this. I hold more stock than any other employee of this company, Fred. You will not tell me what to do!" Russell shouted as he stepped around the table he was seated at.

"You're right, Russell. You don't have to put up with this, and neither do I. You're fired. Get out…," Fred responded before Russell could get completely around the table.

His words stopped Russell in his tracks. He stared at Fred for a few seconds and then he turned and stormed towards the door. As he opened the door and stomped out, Russell could be heard letting loose a string of expletives.

***

As Chris feverishly loaded their notes into Narvell's blog, Narvell finished reviewing the document on the screen in front of him. He then hit the **Print** button on the screen and started printing a copy of the slides for each of them.

"Okay Chris. I think I like it. Have you found anything?"

"Nope. Just finishing with the blog. Go ahead and send it to Schmidt… Done. Want to go over it one last time?"

"Yep. I'm e-mailing it now."

And with that, the two young men began to review the document (See Appendix A for full document).

When they were both finished reviewing it, Chris looked up at Narvell. "I think you've nailed it, Narv. Now all we have to do is convince Schmidt and my father that this is the way to sell it to your management team."

"No. We have one other hurdle to address. We've got to convince your grandfather to tell the tale. I truly think his story about the tape measure will sway any fence straddlers we run into. I'm pretty sure from what we learned in school that there will be a percentage that don't want to change no matter what we say or do, and that there will be others in the room hungry for change. It's the ones in the middle that we have to win over. But, I think we're as ready as we're going to get. Let's call it a day. I'll see you in the morning." And with that closing thought, Narvell closed his laptop, placed it and the printed copy of their presentation in his backpack, stood up, and headed for the door.

Chapter 14

Help from Others

October 5

Narvell had barely slept Tuesday night. No matter what he had tried, nothing could shut out the thoughts of what this meeting might be like. As he walked into Fred's office, a lump formed in his throat. Looking around the outer office, he quickly saw Chris in the corner reading the newspaper. Pat was sitting at her desk with her eyes glued to the computer screen in front of her. She looked up briefly, smiled, and waved as if to say, "Have a seat," then returned her gaze to the computer. As he walked across the room towards Chris, Narvell realized that his legs were shaking. With every step, the shaking seemed to get worse, which only made the six steps over to the chair next to Chris feel like it was sixty.

Sitting down, Narvell looked at Chris. "Are we really ready for this Chris?" Narvell asked, not even trying to hide the nervousness taking over his entire body.

"You bet. Dad's in there right now. Shouldn't be too long before we're on," Chris replied and went back to reading the newspaper.

When the door opened and Fred stepped out to motion the two young men in, Narvell had a sudden feeling of doom and despair. He didn't quite understand why he was so panicked since Fred had a smile on his face and appeared to be relaxed as Narvell and Chris both stood up and headed into the office.

As they entered Fred's inner office, they saw Chris' father Tom sitting in one of the wingback chairs that formed part of the informal seating area in front of Fred's desk. Narvell was somewhat surprised at where Tom was seated since he had expected them to be sitting at the conference table on the other side of the office. Fred rejoined Tom, taking a seat on a small couch in the same area and motioned for Narvell and Chris to join them.

"Gentlemen, sit down. I believe we have a lot to talk about this morning, and I don't want to waste any of Tom's time. So let's get started," Fred said as he leaned back in his seat. "I read over your presentation last night. Very impressive. I've got a few questions, as I think Tom does. But, overall I like it."

With the opening words from Fred, Narvell's panic began to ease some. For some reason, though, he still felt like the hammer was going to come crashing down on his head at any moment. Realizing that this was his presentation and that Chris was there assisting him, Narvell spoke up. "Thank you, Fred. How do you want to do this? Should we go through it slide by slide, or do you want to just dive into the questions?"

"Let's just start with a few questions. First, why do you believe that I have to acknowledge that I don't look at the metrics on the network?"

"Honestly sir, it comes down to the fact that I've been through the entire folder on the server that is supposed to hold copies of the company metrics, and the only numbers online are Rob Allison's. I couldn't find any other team or department numbers anywhere. For you to admit that you haven't been looking at them should, in theory, make it alright for others to openly discuss what's not there and why. It appears to Chris and me that the entire management team, except for Rob, has been negligent on this point."

"Fair enough. I like your thinking. And … you're right. I wasn't even aware that the folders were largely empty until you said something. Okay, next question: why do we want to talk about Housholder Sprockets? Isn't this about us?"

"Fred, I'm not trying to be a smart-ass here, but don't you think we need to address the elephant in the room … namely Chris? I mean if he's going to be here helping me, shouldn't everyone understand why we have someone from Housholder helping us? Think about it, less than a month ago, we had members of the management team talking about corporate spying and sending someone into Housholder, and now … here they are," Narvell said as he realized that the nervousness was gone. As he paused, waiting for a response from Fred, he noticed that his CEO suddenly had a guilty look on his face.

Tom also noticed the look. "Fred, don't worry about it. The espionage thought is not a problem for us. Actually, it's kind of flattering."

"Thank you, Tom. But I do think I owe you and your company an apology. Desperate times do evoke some strong, if not always ethical, ideas."

Fred looked straight at Tom as he said this. In response, he received a nod from Tom.

Then Tom spoke up. "Okay Narvell, next question: Why the tape measure story? And more importantly … Who's going to tell it?"

Before Narvell or Chris could answer, Fred jumped back in. "Look, I understood it when you told it to me. But, it was not an easy sell. What makes you think you can convince our entire management team? After all, two under-thirty staff members from two very different manufacturing companies telling a tale like this may create more chaos than we saw the last two days. I'm struggling with this one."

Chris responded before Narvell had a chance to say anything. "Fred, this one was my idea. I don't think either one of us should tell the story." Looking over at Tom, Chris continued, "I think that granddad should be there to tell it. It's his story, and who better to make the point about how you get everyone involved than the guy that came up with the idea in the first place. Fred, can you give us insight into what happened this week so we can prepare my grandfather?"

Fred looked over at Chris' father. "This may be asking too much of you all, Tom. I can't ask you all to do that."

Setting Fred's mind at ease, Tom responded quickly. "Fred, I've already told you that this is what we do as a company. We are committed to the community and to the manufacturing industry. If Max is what is needed to help turn your problems around, I can assure you that he will have no problem coming in and telling his story."

Fred's response to this was open and honest, if not a bit surprising. "Well, okay. To be honest, the last two days of meetings were not entirely bad. Unless you count one of our longest tenured sales managers getting furious about the whole thing, getting fired, and then storming out of the room cussing. Other than that, I'd say it was a pretty typical, tense type of meeting for a company suffering through a tough stretch."

At Fred's statement about someone storming out, Narvell and Chris gave each other a quick glance as they both recalled Narvell's dream. While neither one said anything about it, a silent connection was made, and both of them contemplated just how serious this adventure was becoming.

Not waiting for Fred to continue, Narvell launched into an explanation of what Chris and he thought would happen after the tale was told. "Fred, we really think that this will set the stage for us explaining the chart we've included. We don't expect that even Max telling the tale, himself, will convince everyone. But we need to get enough people's attention to kick-start some positive change.

"We need for you to co-lead the discussion to reset, or in our opinion, set the KPIs for the company. I hope Max will agree to help with that as well. Then we can start drilling down one level at a time," Narvell concluded.

Chris picked up the explanation at that point. "One thing that I've learned from my father and grandfather is that not everyone will be *on the bus* with you, and many who are *on the bus won't be in the right seats*. It appears to me as an outsider that Jim Collins[*] could have been describing M.E. Burdette Co. when he talked about building bureaucratic rules to manage a small percentage of people on the bus. Looks to me as if M.E. Burdette has had more than its share of the wrong people on the bus over time, which has increased the bureaucracy just to handle this small number of disconnected employees.

"And if that's truly the case, we can't expect everyone to play nice as we move forward. We're talking about culture change. We need some seasoned veterans, you and Max, to get it started and then we pilot the idea as we drill down with willing participants. We know that there is already one believer on board, Rob Allison. We can use him to help us spread the concept."

Narvell wrapped up what Chris had started. "In short, we don't expect this to be easy. Actually, we expect that there will be plenty of hand grenades tossed at us as we try to implement this approach to measuring success. That's why we need it to start with you, Fred. And hopefully, Max will help us get this launched in the right way. So … What other questions do you have for us?"

"Just one, Narvell. Can you two be ready to run with this on Monday? We can't lose any more time. We have got to see some results this quarter. Or worse case scenario is Q1 next year, which means we need to be seeing something inside of six months," Fred said, staring at Narvell, now trying to see if there were any chinks in his armor.

"I believe we are ready, sir. We just need to talk to Max and make sure he's available. Chris, can you handle that detail for us?" Narvell said, standing up. Chris nodded in the affirmative, before Narvell continued, "Now then, where, or should I say what, do you want me to do until Monday, Fred?"

"Why don't you and Chris keep working out of the office you've been using at Housholder, if that's okay with you, Tom. I'll call Rob Allison and have him come back into town tomorrow. I want him to work on a list of

---

[*] Collins, Jim. 2001. Good to Great, *Why Some Companies Make the Leap…and Others Don't.* New York: HarperCollins.

managers that may be more receptive to what we are going to do. I'd like to have the skids greased before we spring this on the management team. Any final thoughts, Tom?"

"Just one. And I want everyone in the room to think about this. There is no magic bullet. You may start on this today, or next week. But do not, I repeat, do not expect fast results. Six months may not be enough time. You should see signs of recovery if you get enough people to buy into the idea. But, I don't want you to think that you'll be back to the very profitable company you once were in only six short months. Culture change is tough. And changing the way you measure success, measure anything for that matter, is even tougher."

And with a nod of the head from all three of the other participants in the room, this meeting was over.

***

Throughout the remainder of the week, Narvell and Chris discussed and debated as many scenarios as they could think of about what might happen come Monday morning. One idea kept coming up: what if there is another blow up like the one that had happened already? Were either one of these two young men, barely starting their careers, ready to do battle with seasoned veterans? In the end, they decided that only time would tell. And they both hoped out loud several times that if something this dramatic were to occur, it needed to happen when Max was there, or at the very least when Fred was leading the discussion on KPIs.

Narvell tried several times Thursday and Friday evening to call Annie. Each time, he was met with voice-mail, which gave no indication of where she was or what she was doing. Finally, on Saturday morning he got a text message from her. In the text, she said that there was definitely tension in the air after Fred's meetings on Monday and Tuesday and a lot of speculation about what Fred and the board were going to do to turn things around. She went on to say that there were even rumors that several of the long time managers were out lobbying their friends on the board to replace Fred. Annie closed out her text by telling Narvell to stay focused, and that she would see him Monday evening after the big meeting.

***

Monday morning found Narvell, Chris, and Max meeting Fred shortly after 7:30 a.m. in Fred's office. While both Max and Chris seemed calm and collected, Narvell was wearing his anxiety on his sleeve. Fred also appeared a bit apprehensive, but his voice was strong as he explained his agenda for the day.

"I had Pat set up the corporate training room for the day. She reserved it for the entire week, should we need it. Your slide presentation is loaded on the computer and a wireless remote is sitting on the podium. After I introduce you all, I'll recap why we are here and then I plan on coming down fairly strong on the management team for not bringing any solutions of consequence to the table. I expect one or two grumblings from the crowd based upon the rumor mill last week. But that's okay. I'll deal with it. Then I will explain why you three are here and then turn it over to you, Narvell. By the way, just so you don't have a shocked look on your face when I introduce you, I will be calling you a management analyst assigned to the office of the CEO. Any questions? If not, let's go."

As they walked down the hallway towards the corporate training room, which was located on the same floor as Fred's office, all four men were aware that several people they passed in the hall seemed to freeze and stare at the sight of Fred and Narvell escorted by a twenty-something-year-old man and one other very distinguished gentleman who appeared old enough to be Fred's father. When they entered the training room, the room went silent almost at once. There were a few whispers in the back of the room but even those faded quickly. As Narvell looked around, he found Bill Cooke sitting at the second row of tables almost dead center in the middle. When Bill saw Narvell, the look on his face immediately conveyed his confusion. He stared at Narvell almost as though he was trying to figure out who this vaguely familiar face was. The longer he stared, the more confused he seemed to be.

Fred opened the meeting by thanking everyone for attending and then passed along a few comments of encouragement from the board. He then stopped himself and turned towards the three men who had escorted him into the room. "Before we go any further, I need to make some introductions. To my left is Mr. Max Housholder, chairman of the board at Housholder Sprockets. On my right is one of Mr. Housholder's up and coming young managers, Mr. Chris Anselmo. And next to Chris is one of our own employees, and our new management analyst assigned to my office, Narvell Mann. Max and Chris have graciously offered to help us address our recent financial issues from an outsider's perspective. They will be assisting Mr. Mann as he begins the process of implementing a series of changes to the way we manage our business."

As soon as Fred said Narvell's name, the look on Bill Cooke's face went from confusion to anger. As soon as he heard the name, it all clicked. Now he was sitting there on the second row staring at the person he thought he had fired two weeks before. There was no hiding the anger on his face. The longer he stared, the redder his face became. Fred also noticed the expression on Bill's face, but kept right on with his planned remarks. "Now, before I turn the floor over to Narvell and Chris, does anyone have any questions?"

Bill almost didn't let Fred finish the question. "As a matter of fact, I do. What is this kid doing here, Fred? I fired him two weeks ago. He shouldn't even be in the building."

With Bill's question and statement, the room immediately came alive with muffled conversation. Many of the managers in the room had no idea who Narvell was or why Bill would make such a statement. As if he had prepared for this exact reaction from Bill, Fred responded without any hesitation. "Bill, let me say this one more time. Narvell is working for me, in my office. What you may think you did, or what you think should be happening right now does not matter. If you cannot respect the team that I have put together to help us with this financial problem, you don't have to stay. The door is right there. Do I make myself clear?"

Fred's response was delivered in an almost icy tone ... a tone that no one in this room had ever heard out of Fred before. It had the effect Fred was hoping for. The room went silent once more. Even Bill froze at what Fred had said. As the full impact of the statement sunk in, Bill settled back into his chair. The expression of anger on his face slowly turned to one of embarrassment as he realized that everyone in the room was staring at him. Fred returned the meeting to the transition point once more. "Now, if there aren't any more questions, Narvell, you and Chris have the floor."

"Thank you, Fred." Narvell said as he stepped to the side of the screen at the front of the room. The first slide of their presentation was now visible on the screen. "Chris and I, along with some assistance from Max Housholder, are going to walk you through a presentation that is intended to get each of you thinking about how we measure success at M.E. Burdette. We are going to challenge you with questions about our current metrics; about how involved our employees are in the measurement process; and, what we must do to not only survive, but to succeed and grow. The one thing that we ask is that you allow us to present. There are places within the presentation where feedback, questions, and other appropriate interaction is not only allowed, but in some instances required. Please use the times where we ask for questions and feedback appropriately. We ask that you not interrupt us during the rest of the presentation; otherwise, we may not get finished on time, or at all. Alright, Chris, shall we?"

Chapter 15

Measurements with Meaning

October 10

Measurements with Meaning

How to Focus on Success

"We want to start this presentation by way of some background information. Specifically, what brought Chris, Max, and I together with Fred in the first place. After Fred met with Engineering several weeks ago to discuss the financial situation of the company, I thought that I needed to understand what metrics were being used to measure success. As the new guy in the room, I really didn't know too much about what was being measured and who was involved in the measuring," Narvell started out. His voice sounded nervous once more as he began the presentation.

The only thing he could think of to do to keep from completely losing it was to stare straight at Jimbo. To his surprise, as he found Jimbo sitting in the third row, Jimbo was staring back with a slight grin on face. When Jimbo realized Narvell was looking straight at him, the older man winked as if to say that it was all right. However, even the familiar face of the man he had turned to many times over the past few weeks didn't completely calm Narvell down. But it was enough to keep him going. "I found the Big Board by the main break room and began to try and understand what exactly it was saying. What I found, initially, appeared to be an incredible amount of very good information." At that statement, Narvell noticed that many of the heads in the room nodded in agreement.

"But … to my surprise, after I had finished going through a considerable amount of data, I had to admit that I had no idea what it all meant collectively." And at that moment, almost every single head in the room quit nodding. All that is, except Rob Allison's. Narvell saw the lone head at the back of the room and realized that he had another friend in the room. Knowing that Rob was also in the room seemed to calm the fear in the pit of Narvell's stomach just a bit as he wrapped up the introduction. Of course, he couldn't see Chris, Fred, or Max, who were all three off to the side out of his peripheral vision.

"Over a casual dinner with Chris, a college roommate of mine, I came to understand just how much I didn't know. Chris asked me some very good questions to ask and eventually I wound up in Fred's office answering some questions, and asking many of the same ones that Chris had asked me. And then Fred asked Chris and me to carry this conversation to the entire management team, to see if we couldn't answer all of the questions that presented themselves to Fred and me through Chris and Max."

And with that, Narvell used the remote on the podium in front of him to change to the next slide.

How Are You Measuring Success Today?

- What measurements are in place currently?

  For the whole company... not just your team or department?

- So what about your team / department?

  – How do you measure success at this level?
  – Why?

- How does this benefit the shareholders?

2

"So the first question we want to discuss is very simple. What measurements are in place today? How do we measure success on the company level today at M.E. Burdette?" Narvell asked and looked around the room. What surprised him were the smiles on quite a few faces, including both Rob and Jimbo.

Allyson spoke up first, and without hesitation. "That's simple. Actually, too simple. I hope you're going somewhere with this quickly. I have a mountain of work to finish and it's not getting done while I'm sitting here with a couple of snot-nosed kids trying to solve the problems of a well-oiled machine."

Chris, who had been standing off to Narvell's left, stepped forward. "Ma'am, if it's so simple, please feel free to elaborate. I'm not an employee here and believe me when I say that I have much more important things to do than to be here helping you. I have an entire company of my own to learn about. So … please do tell. How do *you* measure success at the company level?"

At Chris' opening comment and question, Allyson recoiled slightly, partly from the direct attack and partly out of surprise. She hadn't expected either of these two young men to be anywhere nearly this aggressive. When she had gathered her thoughts, she answered Chris' question. "As I said, simple. We measure sales and the bottom line on the P&L."

Narvell was beginning to feel a bit more at ease when he realized that Chris was definitely all in on this adventure. So, before Chris said anything else, Narvell jumped back into the conversation. "Allyson, where do we find those two numbers on the Big Board? Isn't that where we post our metrics to show how well we are doing?"

"What do you mean where?" Allyson asked with a little irritation in her voice.

"Where exactly on the Big Board are those two numbers posted? I don't recall seeing either one," Narvell fired back, trying to keep his voice in check so it wouldn't seem too aggressive.

"Narvell, why would you ask such a basic question? If this is about getting answers, why didn't you just ask me about the sales totals or bottom line?" a voice from the far side of the front row said. As Narvell turned towards the voice, he recognized the face it belonged to, the company's CFO, Matthew Ward.

"Mr. Ward, that's not exactly the point," Narvell replied. "If we post all these metrics on the board that say how good we are, or bad as the case may be, then the question is … if measuring sales and the bottom line is how we do it at the top, why are they not on the board?"

Before Matthew Ward could respond, Allyson chimed in with a somewhat condescending voice. "All you have to do is add up each region's sales numbers if you can't find the total on the board. And why would we post the bottom line out there? Floor employees don't need to know what the bottom line is. That information is for the shareholders."

"Thank you, Allyson," Chris interrupted. "I believe you've made our point. Narvell, you want to move on?"

"Okay, let's talk about the metrics used by each department and team. "How do you measure success at this level?" Narvell said bringing focus back to the slide on the screen behind him.

"Oh come on, Fred! Do we really need this?" Bill spoke up looking directly at Fred over on the far right side of the room. "Why are we discussing what each and every one of us in this room knows? This is just a waste of time. Every single department has metrics that have proven over and over again how successful, or not, a department is. Just go look at the Big Board if you don't know what we measure. It's all there."

Fred started to respond to Bill's outburst. But, just before the first word came out of his mouth, Narvell stepped directly into the line of sight between the two men and responded. "Bill, humor us for just another few minutes. Then, if you don't like where this is going, maybe Fred will excuse you to do something else with your time. You say that every department has their numbers on the Big Board. Okay, great. So tell me how your numbers, as in Engineering, not anyone else, how do your metrics benefit the shareholders?" Narvell finished this statement with authority in his voice. As he thought about it, he wasn't sure if it was because he was getting over the jitters he had started with, or because he was already tired of the attitude that Bill and Allyson were throwing at him and Chris.

"What do you mean, how does it benefit the shareholders?" Bill said as his voice began to get louder and his face redder.

"Just that, sir. How do all the things you measure in Engineering and post to the Big Board benefit our shareholders? Do they? Do any of them?"

Chris, realizing that the interaction they were having was keeping them on top of the discussion, joined in. "Bill, we are not saying that there is anything wrong with the things you are measuring—at least, not at this point. We are simply trying to understand which metrics you use are actually beneficial to the stockholder."

Bill didn't even try to continue the discussion. Instead, he stood up and slammed his notebook shut. But, before he could even take one step, Fred had stepped forward and back into the activities of the moment. "Bill," Fred said in a very icy tone. "Unless you want to join Russ in the unemployment line, I strongly suggest you sit down and listen to these gentlemen."

Bill was clearly caught between a rock and a hard place. He looked at Fred and saw the icy stare looking back at him. He then looked at both Narvell and Chris. Both of the young men looked back with blank expressions. This was one of the scenarios that they had discussed over and over in the days leading up to today. They knew that the best response was to not respond at all. They had bet on the fact that Fred would be there to disarm such a situation, and he had been. Their response was to not provoke those involved any further. And, it appeared to work. After a short pause that seemed to last forever, Bill sat back down.

From the back of the room, a voice interrupted the silence. "Explain what you mean by *benefits our stockholders*, please." It was Rob Allison. A softball question had been lobbed their way. Nice timing, too.

"Sure thing, Rob," Narvell said looking Rob's way. "For any and all measurements that you report out to the entire company, how does any one of them … or all of them, even … how do they directly affect what is important to our stockholders?

Rob's slight grin was visible as he spoke once more. "So you're asking me what does my team do, and how do we show it, that impacts the stockholder? What does impact the stockholder?"

"A return on their investment, of course. Ultimately, they want to know what we're doing that gets them the return they are looking for. So, what metrics do you have in place that handle that, Rob?"

"The only three I report are on the Big Board: sales dollars, gross margin, and cost of sales as a percentage of sales revenue. Seems to me that each of these is beneficial to the shareholder. What do you think?" Rob replied somewhat rhetorically. And it got the reaction he was hoping for. Immediately others in the room started talking among themselves, asking about the metrics they were using. The person sitting next to Rob leaned over and quietly said something to Rob. Rob glanced up very quickly and grinned at Narvell, then returned to the conversation he had just been drawn into.

Chris and Narvell looked at each other as the quiet conversation grew louder. Chris looked around at his grandfather. Max had a smile on his face showing his acceptance of the way this was going, as early in the day as it was. Max then motioned to Chris to keep the presentation moving along. Chris, in turn, motioned to Narvell to change the slide. Narvell obliged him, and then Chris stepped up next to the podium and began to speak as he changed to the next slide.

What about the Employees?

- Do employees know if the company is successful?
    - How?
    - Which employees?
- Do employees know if they are successful?
    - How?
- Does each employee know how their work specifically impacts the "measurements"?

3

"Okay everyone … I recognize that this last question has evoked some conversation, all good, I hope. But, we've got to keep things moving along. So, let me ask another question: what about your employees? How do they know if they are successful? For that matter, how do they know if the company is successful?"

"We tell them," came a voice from the left side of the training room.

Chris looked in that direction. "What *do* you tell them … exactly?"

"We tell them that they are doing a good job … or not, depending on what kind of a job they are doing."

"A bit arbitrary isn't it?" Chris said, looking directly at the person now.

"What do you mean? Either they're doing a good job or they're not. Sounds pretty simple to me," the man said as he leaned forward in his chair.

"Maybe too simple," said Narvell, joining the conversation. "How often do you tell each and every one of your employees how they are doing?"

"Well … at a minimum they are guaranteed to hear it at their performance review each year," the man said and laughed at his rather weak attempt to be humorous. However, numerous other people in the room chuckled with him, showing Narvell and Chris that they were nowhere near winning over their audience

Chris saw an opening and jumped. "Thank you for making our point for us. If the only time an employee knows how he is doing, good or bad, is when you as managers say something, or worse yet … saying it only once a year during performance reviews, then what are you really accomplishing?" Chris raised his hand as if to say *Don't speak, I'm not done*. Then he continued his point. "And more importantly, how do they know that what they are doing truly has an impact on the success of the company?

"Measurements alone will not accomplish anything. How people are measured drives their behaviors. When people become focused on the right measurements and know how they impact them, they focus on and start working on the right things to achieve the stated goals and objectives. And in the end, accountability to the measurements must be explained and enforced for all of this to work. I think as Narvell continues to go through this, you will see what we mean. Narvell, care to move on?"

"Thanks, Chris," Narvell said with growing confidence. Chris' ability to shut down the talk and mild attacks gave Narvell some self-assurance that the two of them did indeed know what they were talking about. Changing to the next slide, Narvell was now ready to ask some very loaded questions of the managers in the room.

So Let's Recap M.E. Burdette's Metrics

- Over 300 metrics are on the Big Board by the main break room.
- Who in this room reads the metrics posted?
  - Every single one of them?
  - No? Then which ones?
  - Why?
- Who thinks any employee reads them all?
- Who thinks any employee reads any of them?
- If employees read them, do they know what they mean and how they impact them?

4

"Let's shift gears for a moment and talk about the metrics on the Big Board outside of the break room. I've read through them with great interest. Who else in this room has read all of them?" Narvell asked, hoping to set someone up to get to the root of the problem.

Several hands went up around the room. Narvell turned and looked straight at Bryan Steinman from Engineering and then paused for effect before continuing. "Bryan, that's great. So, you've read through all the metrics on the Big Board? Every single one?"

"Well, no. Not all of them. But I have read Engineering's."

"That's not what I asked. I asked who has read *all* of them. Anyone? Fred, what about you? Have you read them all?" Narvell asked, spinning on his heel and facing the CEO.

"Well, no. As a matter of fact, I haven't. I suspect that there isn't anyone in this room that has read them all, except maybe you. Am I right?" Fred's response was right on target and punctuated with just the right amount of pop to surprise the entire room. And the way he looked out across the room, searching for someone to prove him wrong, added to the confessional moment. Not a single person moved with the question, which allowed Narvell and Chris to continue without interruption.

Chris took over the presentation and delivered the closing line for the slide in front of the room. "So then, if they aren't being read and utilized to understand how the company is doing, what are they really accomplishing? In other words, if the only thing anyone reads is their own department's numbers, why post them all together anyway? Narvell told me that it took him over an hour, uninterrupted, just to read what was on the board. Does anyone want their employees to spend that much time looking at a wall of numbers all the time? No answers or comments, please. Just think about it."

"Who knows where your metrics that are shown on the Big Board are kept on the network?" Chris asked, and then nodded at Narvell to take over.

So Let's Recap M.E. Burdette's Metrics

- Who knows where the metrics are kept on the network?

- How many of you have looked at them on the network?

- What's the purpose for all these numbers if we can't use them to measure our success and pinpoint our opportunities?

5

Narvell watched as most of the people in the room raised their hands. Several more nodded to confirm their knowledge on the subject. "So then, how many of you have looked at any other department or team's metrics on the network?"

Bill Cooke and Bryan Steinman both raised their hands, along with several others. Narvell, thinking it wise not to pick on Bill again without risking another altercation, looked over at Bryan. "And whose have you looked at, Bryan?"

"All the Engineering team's plus several of the sales team's," Bryan said very confidently.

"And when was the last time you did this, if you don't mind me asking?"

"Well, uh …. Seems to me it was fairly recently. I can't really give you an exact date," Bryan replied as he became aware that everyone in the room was now staring at him.

Narvell let Bryan's answer hang in the air for a moment and then he turned towards Fred once more. "Fred, have you been reviewing the metrics stored on the network?"

"Actually, I think I'm going to come clean on this topic as well. I don't recall ever looking at any of the metrics on the network. At least not since the idea was rolled out and presented at a management retreat four or five years ago. Why do you ask?" Fred almost couldn't keep the smile from his face as he finished his answer. It was as if Narvell and Chris had scripted exactly what they needed to have happen and everyone in the room had played their parts perfectly. Not a head turned, or a mouth made any sound as Fred answered and looked at Narvell, anticipating the answer that was about to be dropped on the CEO in front of the entire management team of the company.

"Well sir, after I looked at the Big Board until my eyes were almost crossed, I thought it might be easier to review them on the network. Jimbo told me where to look and I went out to the server and started going through the folders on the metrics drive. To my surprise, there were folders for each department, and folders in folders for almost every team. But the one thing that was missing was the files with metrics. Wait …. That's not quite fair. Actually, Rob Allison's team metrics were the only ones on the entire drive. And I guess you could say that HR was close. The HR department at least had files in their folders that said to go look at the Big Board for their measurements. And I must confess that many of the folders were not even accessible. I was locked out for security reasons."

Fred was beginning to feel like a member of Narvell's team as he added on to the end of Narvell's statement. "But I wasn't. After we talked in my office, and you explained what all you had done and what needed to be said, I went out and looked in every single folder. I wasn't locked out of any of them. And guess what? There was nothing in any of them. So, it appears as though, with one exception …" Fred said nodding towards Rob, "we are all guilty of not doing what we agreed to do in regards to our measurements. Please continue, gentlemen."

Narvell started in once again on the topic at hand. "The point in all of this is that it does us no good to post data, heck … even collect it for that matter … if we aren't going to use it. How do we know how good or bad we are if we are all living in a vacuum? Perhaps we need to step back for a moment and look at the bigger picture," Narvell said and turned towards the next slide on the screen.

Why Are We Here?

- Why does M.E. Burdette Co. exist?
- If the company doesn't make money, how can it survive?
- Then what?
    - What would M.E. Burdette Co.'s employees do?
    - What would you all, the management team, do?
- So, if everyone knows why we are here, who can explain why nearly every department is sub-optimizing?

6

"Why are we here? Not as individuals, I think we all get that, right .... We have to have a job to make money to pay for a house and cars and utilities and kids. What I mean is, why does M.E. Burdette exist? The answer is simple: to make a profit. If the company can't make money, why should it exist at all? If we can't turn this around, what are you all as managers going to do? Where are you going to find a job? Do you really want to go through that? And, what about the employees? How many of them would suffer? Some of our production workers have been here for over twenty years I've been told. Really? If it's all about the company making money, and in turn providing a decent living for employees and managers alike, then why are you all acting as if only your area of the company matters?

"Each of you has your own goals and objectives and you post the results to the board in the hall. Each of you, and your teams, are focused on being successful, but only as a single team. I spent days going over the results on the Big Board, and initially I just kept saying why, if we are so good, are we in trouble? It made absolutely no sense. Then I started discussing it with Chris, and it started to get a bit clearer. It appears as though almost every team and department in the company, and possibly even each individual, is suboptimizing the processes to reach team and department goals, all at the expense of other teams and departments."

Bill couldn't contain the anger that had welled up inside of him any longer. He stood up and looked at Narvell, and then Chris, and finally at Fred. The red in his face was almost as bright as the red coffee cup in front of him. "I've had enough. I don't know about the rest of you, but I don't need some twenty-one-year-old kid telling me how to do my job. I've worked here longer than you've been alive. I know what works and what doesn't. You don't have a clue what you're talking about."

"Bill," Fred stepped up next to Narvell and Chris as he spoke.

"Fred. Not now. I want to talk to you alone about this. I am not going to sit here and be accused of making others fail, so I can look good. When this charade is over, I'll be in my office." And with that, Bill Cooke walked out of the meeting.

Before Fred could say anything else, Max appeared right beside him. In a quiet tone, almost a whisper, Max said to Fred, "Let him go. You might even ask if anyone else wants to join him. If they do, let them leave. You can deal with them later."

Fred, with an odd look on his face, glanced at Max. What he saw was experience. Max had a calm collected demeanor that was very reassuring in the moment. So, Fred did just as Max had suggested. "Anyone else want to leave. Please feel free to. I'll meet with you and Bill after we're done here." Not one single person moved. Not an inch. Not even Bryan Steinman. "Very well. Sorry for the interruption. So what do we do, gentlemen? I know I didn't bring you in here to just talk about what we are doing wrong."

It was now Chris' turn to lead the presentation. Narvell handed Chris the remote and took a step backward. As Chris clicked the remote to change the slide, he said, "It appears that we may have a dilemma here."

The Dilemma!

What do we do?

Business as usual? Or do we change the model?

7

"What do you do? Business as usual? Try to ignore what's happening? … Follow in Bill's footsteps and keep on as you have been … as if nothing's wrong? Or do you look around and find a new business model? Why not change the playing field? As Albert Einstein said: "Insanity: doing the same thing over and over again and expecting different results." Is that what M.E. Burdette Company has become? So … What do you do? How about looking around for that new business model? You don't have to reinvent the wheel here. There are plenty of successful companies that you can look toward to help you find the answer."

What Do the Best of the Best Do?

- Apparently we are not the best of the best in town, much less the state, country, or industry.

- To be successful, you must always look around you at both success and failure.

- Right here in town we have an example of success.

  – Housholder Sprockets
  – Industry leader, community leader, profitable

8

"How many of you would say that you are the best manufacturer in your industry?" Chris waited, but no one said a word or even raised a hand. Trying to lighten the mood, Chris added, "This is the time when we want you to participate." And then he laughed softly. At this comment, Rob and several others in the back of the room raised a hand, along with three others seated in front. "Okay. Now we're getting somewhere. How many of you think you are the best manufacturer in town?"

"From your slide, it's pretty apparent that you all don't think we're the best," Bryan said in a rather sarcastic tone. This comment actually drew quite a number of laughs.

"You're right, Bryan, we don't. But only because of the financial condition the company is in. If this was just about the product, I think it would be a different discussion," Narvell interjected.

"Narvell's right," Chris continued. "The product is great, but the company is struggling. Instead of trying to reinvent that wheel, or think radically outside the box, what should a company do? You've got to look around you at both success and failure. Look inside your industry. Look within your own community. When was the last time any of you visited another manufacturer? Any manufacturer, anywhere.

"Well … today you don't have to go anywhere to hear what makes a successful manufacturer good. Instead, a successful manufacturer has come to you. I'd like to turn the meeting over to Max Housholder, Chairman of Housholder Sprockets. Max."

 A Tale of Success

The Tape Measure

9

Chapter 16

A Time to Start Over

"In closing, let me make one final statement: Each of you in this room needs to find your tape measure. Find your sixteenth of an inch. Then connect the dots. You'll see how it fits with the eighth of an inch, and then the quarter, half, and then the inch. As you move up your corporate structure, you'll then start seeing how all the inches fit together to form a foot and more. If you don't figure out how to tie the entire organization together through measurement, you will never be able to sustain success. That's probably the biggest reason why you are where you are today.

"I do want to thank you for letting me tell my story about the tape measure without interruption. I can see from more than a few faces that many of you don't believe what I said. And that's okay. There has to be a devil's advocate on every team to challenge all of us if we're going to keep getting better. The only thing I ask is that all of you keep an open mind. Again, thank you." And with those final words, Max Housholder turned and walked back over to the corner of the room where Fred had been standing.

Max had just completed telling the history of Housholder Sprockets and the story of the tape measure without a single person interrupting. The room had gone almost deathly quiet when Max spoke his first word, and it had stayed that way throughout his talk. Narvell had been as engrossed in Max's story as everyone else in the room, even though he had heard it all before. What struck Narvell as truly amazing was that the tape measure story, as told by Max, was nearly identical to the way Chris had told it to him. The only real difference was that this version was a first person narrative.

Before Narvell could stand up and return to the podium, an interesting thing happened. Something occurred that Narvell and Chris, and even

Fred for that matter, had not really thought about when planning the day out. Applause. It started with Rob Allison, but was quickly picked up by the newer members of the management team. And then slowly nearly every person in the room was clapping. Max raised a hand in acknowledgement and then pointed at Narvell and Chris. In response, the applause trickled to a halt.

As the room quieted down, Narvell took charge once more. "Thank you, Max. I hope that we as a company can find our tape measure. I truly believe that through this process, we can find what's wrong and make it right. To do that, we've proposed to Fred that it might be time to completely start over with how we measure success at M.E. Burdette." Narvell then punctuated his statement by changing the slide.

Time to Start Over

- Create measurements with meaning.
  - Structured from top to bottom within the organization.
  - Everyone in the company MUST know if we are successful or not.
- A few simple measurements at each level of the company can accomplish this.
  - This doesn't mean you don't measure other things.
  - The metrics you post are all linked together.

10

"To do this, Fred has agreed that we need to follow Max's advice and develop a measurement system that is truly linked from the top of the company to the bottom; each and every employee must understand the system. That everyone knows on an ongoing basis if they, and the company, are successful."

Fred walked over and joined Narvell and Chris at the front of the room as Narvell was starting his explanation. He then caught Narvell by surprise when he spoke up well before they had planned for Fred to take over the meeting. "Let me emphasize what Narvell and Chris are saying here. We are going to throw out every single metric currently in place and start over. It doesn't mean that some of the things we measure today won't still be measured. It simply means that we won't clutter up an entire wall with a bunch of numbers that no one can tie together to make any sense."

"What we need are a few simple measurements at every level of the organization that ties every team and department together, through the organizational structure of the company. Ultimately the idea is that each level, from the bottom to the top, feeds into our Key Performance Indicators," Narvell added.

What Success Looks Like

- Start at the top – Key Performance Indicators.
  - Develop 3–4 meaningful KPIs at the top of the organization.
  - Involve stakeholders, managers, and employees alike.
  - Everyone must understand the difference between indicators and goals.

- Top level management MUST be on board … leading this effort!

11

Fred was clearly on board at this point, as he presented his own surprise to the management team. "I've already discussed the issue with the board of directors, and to a person each and every member is in agreement with this approach. As a matter of fact, we met last night and had Max facilitate a session to identify our KPIs. The board, through Max's poking and prodding," Fred chuckled as he said this, "guided us to an interesting conclusion. We believe that there are only three things at the very top of our company that are needed to measure success. (1) Top-Line Growth, (2) Bottom-Line Growth, and, 3) Customer Satisfaction. However, the board directed me to assemble a team of managers to review this and try to poke holes in it. So, when we are done today, I'm going to ask a few people to stay behind. If you're interested in expressing your opinions on the subject, tell me as soon as we're done."

Fred looked at Narvell, now as much for support as to signal him to continue.

"Fred is right about the need for input from this team. You've all got to be involved in the decision-making process to make it work. But maybe even more important is that you need to go back and explain what the board is thinking in regards to these KPIs and get input from your employees. And when we talk about stakeholders, don't forget … that might mean the board, shareholders, managers in your department, and managers in other departments that touch your processes on a regular basis. It definitely means process owners and those key employees that make things happen and also your customers. This has to be a two-way street. You've got to get input from these stakeholders. But, and I'll say this for Fred, if you don't mind, sir, each and every one of *you* has to be on board. If you aren't, this can very easily fail. This may be the single toughest thing for some of you to do. But you must. This is a cultural change that requires support *and* engagement from the very top of the company to the very bottom."

Success – Top Down

- After KPIs are developed at the top, it's time to start filtering down.
- At the next level down …
    - Managers must then develop metrics to feed KPIs.
    - These should be objective based and critical to success.
    - There must also be some employee-based metrics that show the employee/team that they are succeeding.
    - Upper-level managers MUST get their team involved to develop the metrics at this level.

12

"Once the management team agrees on KPIs, it's time to start pushing the concept downhill. At that first level down, we're talking about our four business units .... Sales, Manufacturing, Engineering, and Administrative Services, you need to develop metrics that feed the KPIs. Once again, just like with the KPIs, you only need a few metrics to truly measure success, three or four per area. That means that we'd have twelve to sixteen key metrics at this level feeding up into the KPIs. Internally to each of these business units, there may also be other measurements that very clearly show the employees how they are doing. These additional measurements should be displayed within the business unit, but not reported upstream as a general rule. As you establish these metrics, you've got to get your employees involved. Not only do they have to understand what you're going to be measuring, they've got to have ownership in them and know how their work impacts these measurements. Setting the measurements at this level is critical to the success of the system, since these are the numbers that directly feed the KPIs."

What Success Looks Like

- **Further down the organizational chain:**
  - At each level down, management MUST develop metrics that feed upstream towards the KPIs.
  - This is what ties knowledge of success at all levels of the company together.
  - Just as at the higher levels, metrics should be objective based and critical to success.
  - There must also be some employee-based metrics that show the employee/team that they are succeeding.
  - AND, at each level all employees MUST feel ownership in the measurements.
  - Everyone in the organization MUST have their personal success directly linked to meeting these metrics!

13

Chris took over at this point and began to drive the point home about how to spread the concept down through the company. "Once you've got your metrics in place at the business unit level, it's time to really get busy. Each department under your business units must then break out and do the exact same exercise creating their key metrics that feed the business unit metrics above them. Same concept … three or four per department is all you need. But once again, you may need to develop some other measurements to clearly show your employees their success. And just like at the business unit level, there is no reason to report those additional measurements upstream. They should stay within the department. To be quite honest, there is no reason to post any metric at this level upstream with the top-level metrics and the KPIs. Instead, you should be posting the KPIs along with the key metrics from your business unit within your department. Alongside the KPI and business unit metrics display, you then post your department metrics that are feeding the business unit metrics and KPIs. And then finally, you would post any additional measurements that you are using to show employees how successful they are."

To avoid any confusion, Chris stepped to the smartboard on the wall closest to the door and drew a quick sketch of what this would look like.

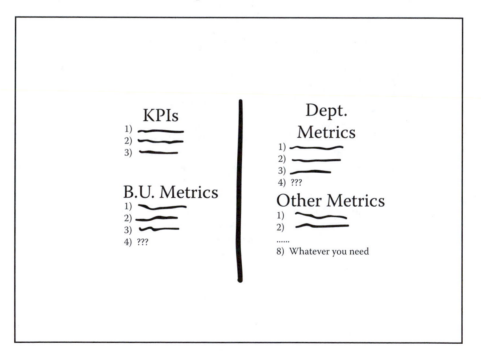

"You don't have to have four metrics at the business unit level. You may do it with three or the number might be five or six …. I really hope it's not six .... You need to try and narrow it down to three or four. It may take a lot of work. Likewise, at the department level shoot for three or four. And then as you develop those additional measurements to help the employees understand how they are doing, try your best to limit these to the smallest number possible. Standardize how you measure your employees for this purpose. I put eight up there, but really, the fewer the better. For most organizations, if you pick the right metrics at the department level, you won't have to even come up with any other measurements for the employees at this level. We're talking about managers and supervisors here, not the rank and file.

"Let me say this again," Chris stated emphatically. *"For most organizations, if you pick the right metrics at the department level, you won't have to have any other measurements at this level. We're talking about managers and supervisors, not rank and file employees."*

Narvell took over to explain how the process continues. "Once you have it at the department level, you can then repeat the entire process going down to the next level of the company. The way you report it out looks exactly the same," Narvell said motioning towards the smartboard. "The only difference is that at the team, or work center level, you replace the business unit metrics on your display with the department. Talking to Max about this strategy, he said that some organizations keep the business unit metrics on the display and add the department metrics alongside. He did caution me though, that it might get too cluttered and busy. Max, I believe you said to be very careful about this, right? Don't get it so busy that you can't read and understand what's going on in just a few minutes?"

"You're absolutely on point, Narvell. If you get too much displayed, whether it's on a wall or on your computer screen, you will very quickly lose your audience. If your employees don't understand what's really going on, they will lose interest in the system, and ultimately the success of the company," Max explained without moving from this spot leaning against the wall.

Narvell changed the slide and immediately noticed that several people in the room started taking notes based upon this new slide.

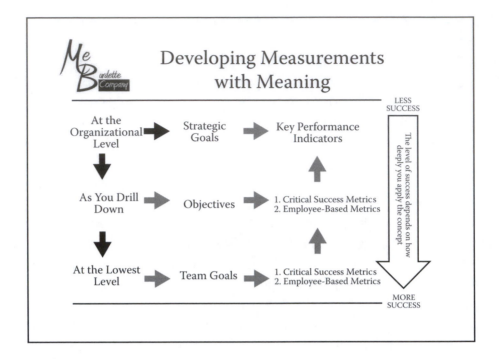

"As you can see from our chart here, the idea is to use the strategic goals of the company to create our KPIs. As you then drill down, level-by-level, you use your business unit objects and then department and/or team goals to create key metrics that are critical for success. Then you develop those additional metrics if you need them. If you'll notice on the right side of the chart, you can see the level of success that you gain as you take the concept deeper into the organization. Those companies that only create KPIs and don't link their measurement system all the way through the organization may be profitable. But, they won't be nearly as successful over the long haul as those that use this methodology to create their measurement system.

"The deeper into the organization you go and more employees who understand what is important, the better off you will be. The more successful you will be. The challenge is to find what's important at every level of the company. Each and every member of the management team has got to find what is most important at their level and then measure it. They've got to find their tape measure," Narvell said with great confidence now. He realized as he said the last statement that he thought he truly understood what Max and Chris had been telling him.

What Success Looks Like

- To truly be successful, employees MUST be engaged!

- Employees have to have ownership in the measurements if you want the effort to succeed culturally.

- There MUST be measurements at each level of the company, from bottom to top, that shows the workforces how they are doing.

- Employees have to be allowed to participate in the creation of some metrics.

15

"A very big challenge for our management team will be breaking the cultural paradigm that we currently live in. While we talk about how this is a top-down effort, you've got to understand that success comes from the bottom up. When every employee, even the newest and lowest paid employee, understands the mission and is committed to that mission ... then you can start creating success from the inside out, from the bottom to the top. And when those same employees are engaged in deciding what you measure, they will feel ownership in the metric. They will feel ownership in the process. Having the metrics displayed prominently in the area where an employee works allows them to see how they are doing on an ongoing basis," Narvell said, and then he looked at Chris to carry on the explanation.

Chris took the remote from Narvell and stepped forward. "When you display your metrics, keep them updated regularly. KPIs should be updated, *at a minimum*, on a quarterly basis. If at all possible, they should be updated monthly. Your business unit metrics should definitely be updated monthly. Departmental and team metrics should, worse case, be updated monthly and many times they can be updated as frequently as weekly. The additional metrics you create to help your employees know how successful they are can be updated anywhere from monthly to every day. The more frequent the updates, the better informed your employees will be …. The better off they'll be. Immediate feedback is an incredible motivator. It's human nature to want to do well, to succeed. Help your employees succeed by telling them how they're doing on an ongoing basis.

"It's important to recognize that what we measure drives behavior, and behavior drives action." As Chris was saying this, he walked back over to the smartboard and erased what was already there. Then, as he spoke he began to write: "The things you measure are a reflection of your organizational values. And these values are the fundamental building blocks that shape your company's vision and action. You measure what you value. Measures directly influence how people work. In turn, how people work affects organizational results. This is a big interlinked circle of events wrapped around the culture of the organization. When we talk about the culture of an organization, this is at the heart of that culture. The organizational values drive what we do as an organization. When we measure what we value, it affects our behavior …. Do you see the circular effect I'm referring to here?"

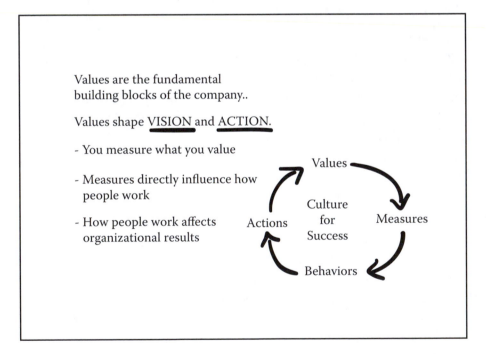

"The next couple of slides that I'm going to show you are what we'll be using to help us confirm the KPIs that Fred discussed earlier, as well as what will guide us as we establish metrics at various levels of the organization."

Then Chris showed two slides, allowing the management team to read through each one.

Where Do We Start?

- At the top!
  - Name the critical items or areas that should be measured that are critical to our success.
  - Reduce the list to the basic measurements that we MUST know.
  - Convert these to indicators, not goals.
  - How often do we measure them?

- These KPIs will guide us through the rest of our journey.

16

Next Steps

- At each level of the organization repeat the same exercise with these changes:
  - Start by sharing the KPIs and explaining what they are and why they are important to the company's success.
  - Share the critical success metrics from the level above and explain why they are important.
  - Now develop your measurements that support and feed the level above and ultimately feed the KPIs.
  - How often do you measure?
  - Don't forget to create some employee-based metrics that show the team their success!

17

"The final step in all of this," Chris continued as he looked over at Fred, "is creating a culture of sustainment. You've got to change the culture in such a way that the process is self-sustaining. What this requires is that you review the KPIs annually for relevance and adjustment if required. Once the KPI review is complete, you've got to review your metrics at every level to ensure that they are still relevant and that they remain linked upward throughout the company and back into the KPIs.

Cultural Sustainment

- Review KPIs annually for relevance.
- After KPI review, start the review process from top to bottom for metrics at each level.
- Celebrate success!
- Learn from Success and Failure!
    - If you fail, determine why! If you succeed, determine why!
    - Sustain the gains (put controls in place and monitor the changes)
    - Communicate results and knowledge obtained
    - Re-evaluate and adjust (if necessary) goals and objectives to meet KPIs

18

There are a couple of other things you need to remember when we talk about sustainment. First, you *must* celebrate success. I can't stress this enough. Everyone in the company needs to know when there is a success story. Second thing to remember, learn from both success and failure. Whether your team succeeds or fails, learn from the experience. Success breeds success. So, make sure you know how you accomplished it. And learning from failure is imperative if you are to succeed over the long haul. As you get better at what you do, and you learn how you do it, you put controls in place so that if you begin to slip, you'll see it faster and can react appropriately. Be sure and spread the word about the successes and lessons learned. Communicate throughout the company, so that other teams and departments aren't recreating the wheel after you've already been through the fire yourself. Create an environment of organizational learning.

As individuals learn, they must share the new knowledge that they have acquired. This is in line with what Peter Senge discussed in his book, *The Fifth Discipline*.* It doesn't matter what it is, measure, or project, or process, if you fail to share the knowledge, you are destined to repeat the discovery. This costs you time and your organization money. And finally, remember that all of this is part of continuous improvement. Evaluate and adjust, review and refocus. The goal is to get better each and every day.

"Narvell, unless you have something to add, I think we can turn this back over to Fred."

---

* Senge, Peter. 1990. *The Fifth Discipline: The Art and Practice of the Learning Organization.* New York: Doubleday/Currency.

Chapter 17

Take 2

Fred had stepped back up to the podium and had explained what was yet to come. After a short break, he had asked Rob Allison and Allyson Leigh from Sales, along with Matthew Ward, the CFO, Dane Peters from Manufacturing, and Jimbo Chisholm from Engineering to return to discuss the next step in the process. Before he dismissed the management team, Fred had backed up what he had said at the beginning of the meeting by adding that anyone else interested in working on Phase Two could come back as well.

What Fred, Chris, and Narvell had not expected is who else would return. When the three men returned to the training room, the five managers they had asked to return were sitting there with all the other managers except one, Bryan Steinman. Narvell thought that perhaps Bryan had decided to join Bill Cooke and find other things to do for the rest of his morning, or day, or life. Every other person had decided to stick around and see what Fred and his team of two young and brash internal consultants had up their sleeves.

Fred motioned to Narvell and Chris to sit in chairs that had been positioned on the front row facing the other people in the room. Fred sat down in the third and final chair, looked around at everyone in the room, and finally spoke. "Thank you. I want to thank each of you for having enough interest in our company to come back for some more of this. I know that we've spent a lot of time focused on this topic over the last month or so. So, it's refreshing to see that so many of you are dedicated enough to hang in there with us.

"I hadn't planned on everyone coming back. And honestly ... what we have planned to kick this off won't require all of you. We need to start small and prove out the methodology. If we can start making some gains over the next few months, we can ramp up what we're doing and expand it as fast as we can handle it. Until then, I want to focus on two areas, and then ... come to think about it ... not all of both areas even to start. I want Jimbo to work with Narvell on Engineering. And I've asked Chris to work with Rob on Sales, one region at a time."

"Fred, what about Bill? Engineering is his baby. Isn't he going to be involved?" asked Matthew.

"Bill got himself a well deserved vacation today. After this meeting, I'm sending him home to think about a few things. I was very disappointed in his actions today. None of you deserved to see that, especially Narvell and Chris. When he comes back, we'll discuss his place in the company. Until then, Jimbo, Engineering is yours."

"Yes, sir!" came the excited reply from Jimbo.

"Now, what are your thoughts about the KPIs?" Fred asked.

Matthew Ward spoke first. "I think I understand the basic premise here. But how do we measure the success of Manufacturing if they don't have a KPI in the game? How do we measure administrative support and its impact without any KPIs focused on support services?"

Jimbo added to the comment without waiting for Fred to respond. "Matt, I hate to say that I agree with a bean counter, but ... I think I agree with you. How are we going to measure Engineering's progress at the top level without a KPI on the board?"

Fred had been waiting for this moment since he had seen the light during his discussions with Max and Tom. "Think about this: What one thing have you been measuring in Engineering that your customer cares about ... at a high level?"

Jimbo sat there staring at Fred for several minutes trying to think of all the Engineering metrics he could remember: number of new products released per year, on time delivery of new products to Manufacturing, meeting deadlines on spec sheets to Marketing. Nope. The more he thought about it, the more Jimbo realized that Engineering's customers were really only interested in one major thing: how quickly did Engineering successfully solve the problem. It's not how did we do against Bill's arbitrary two week deadline for cost analysis requests, as Narvell had pointed out. If we beat the two weeks by one day, it looks great. But why make an employee sit on their work for six days before they give the answer to the customer? What are Sales and Marketing interested in from Engineering? What is our customer in Seattle or Boston interested in when it comes to Engineering? They want answers, specification sheets, drawings, new products, redesigned products—whatever it is that they need is what they expect. And typically, time is of the essence. They want what they want when they want it. That is what Engineering's customers want. As Jimbo sat there thinking about all of this, he suddenly realized that no one else in the room was talking. As he looked around, he saw that everyone was staring at him, even Fred. Then it hit him. Fred had asked him a question and was waiting for an answer.

"Oh sorry, Fred. Got lost in my thoughts there a bit. And you're right. I can't think of a single thing we're measuring in Engineering that our customers actually care about. I think I see where this is going," Jimbo replied with a slight hint of embarrassment on his face.

"Okay. Thanks, Jimbo. Matt, same question to you. What have we been measuring in Manufacturing and on the support side that our customers care about? What metrics are you thinking of that show our success at that level?"

"Fred," Matt replied. "If we aren't measuring things, how do we know how we're doing?"

"Matt, no one said we wouldn't measure. I suspect that we'll probably still be measuring a lot of things we have in the past. But how we use them should change. Instead of driving every single thing we measure to one Big Board, we should be using a lot of the details at a lower level in the company. But … I do hope that many of the metrics we create will be new and fresh. We need to evaluate and align all of our metrics. The point is, we can measure the right things at the right levels and tie them all together to build us a house we can be proud of. Think about it: our shareholders want a profitable business. That's top level, like Max Housholder was saying … They want a house built that looks good and meets their expectations. All the shareholder is interested in is the KPIs, the results, not the details. Next level down, we have metrics in place that show success for the business units at a high level and they also feed the KPIs. This is where customer expectations come into play. We've got to be measuring what's important to the customer. And, it has to be value-added. What I mean by that is that your customer *must* see value in what you are doing. If the customer sees no value, it's a waste. In the lean manufacturing world that waste, that nonvalued thing you're doing, falls into one of the eight wastes categories of lean. So, look for the value-added things your customer is interested in and measure the most important. For Sales, it might be measuring how fast we get price quotes back to the customer and how quickly we can get the product to them. For Shipping, it might be about quality and speed; did we get the right items that meet our quality specs shipped out on time. At this higher level, we are probably talking mostly about our ultimate customers who buy our product—they are out there in the real world along with our shareholders who are looking at us to turn a profit.

"But then we start drilling down. As we go down another level, we get a bit more detailed. Next level, down more, more detailed. And so on, and so on. Some will be using their tape measure to measure in feet, others will measure in inches, and finally some in quarters or even sixteenths of an inch. But ultimately, to build the finest house we can, everyone must tie what he or she is measuring together. It must all fit. And we must stay focused on our customer at every level. We must know what the customer thinks is valuable in what we do. Matt, who's your customer?"

"You. The board. The shareholders. I guess, based upon what you're saying, then some of Accounting's customers would be Engineering, Purchasing, and Manufacturing because if Accounts Payable doesn't pay the bill, we don't get materials we need, right?" Matt asked, starting to see what Fred was referring to.

"You're getting there, Matt. Jimbo, does this make sense to you?" Fred asked, going back to where the discussion started.

"You bet it does. What you've said combined with what Narvell has been talking about, us sitting on work in Engineering instead of sending it on when we are done, paints a fairly clear picture. We've got to ask what our customer wants and needs and translate that into a measurement. It doesn't have to be a lot of things, still only three or four …. But focused on the customer," Jimbo replied, looking around the room and seeing Fred smiling and nodding in agreement.

It was Allyson who spoke next. "I get it … I really think I do. And you have my support and dedication, Fred. Sales will begin implementing immediately. But, Rob hasn't used that mindset with his measurements he's posting on the Big Board. He's only reporting sales dollars, gross margin and cost of sales. How does this fit into your theory, Fred?"

"Well, if I've interpreted what Narvell, Chris, and Rob have been telling me correctly, there is some of this customer focus in his measurements. But, there is probably more that he is not reporting … Rob?" Fred responded without any hesitation.

Rob spoke up just as quickly. "You're right, Fred. If you think about it, our customer wants what they want, when they want it, and at a fair price. So, our ability to respond to that is seen through the sales dollars. If we are giving them what they want when they want it, our sales go up—that is a direct reflection of how well we are meeting their wants and needs. They want it at a fair price. Margin reflects this to some degree. And of course, cost of sales reflects both how much effort we had to put into it and what we had to give away or throw in to get the sale. What you don't see here is what I measure on a team and individual basis: response time to customer requests, whether that's basic info or a quote or an order acknowledgement, sales dollars generated from individual customers, customer satisfaction with the team and/or individual. Much of this is also related to what our customer wants, but we don't need to flood the entire company with details. And if the truth be known, if we are taking care of the three we put on the Big Board, then the rest has a way of taking care of itself."

Allyson was nodding her head in agreement as Rob was explaining all of this. When he had finished, she went back to her endorsement of the idea. "Based upon what Rob just explained and what his team has done up in the Northeast, we can improve a whole lot in a hurry by following his model. Just tell me what you want us to do. I think the KPIs are as close to perfect as we can get them for a first attempt. Let's get this thing going."

"Anyone else have anything to add?" Fred asked as he scanned the room. Waiting to give everyone time to process what had been said, Fred finally continued, "Okay then, let's do this. Since we have so many of us here, everyone from Sales and Marketing huddle up in the back corner over there. Engineering … Jimbo, you and your managers can meet in the small conference room next door with Narvell. And Chris, if you don't mind, how about you meet with me, Matt, and the admin and support managers here in the front of the room.

"We all now know what the KPIs are. So, spend the next hour or so trying to come up with your top level measurements for each strategic business unit. We only want three or four for each business unit, no more. Understood? I'll call Pat and have some pizza or sandwiches brought in. Keep at this until you have what you think are the right measurements. We can all get together and review all of them when we think we're there. People, we are only working on those three or four metrics for the strategic business units. Don't wander off into something else, or go any deeper. And one more thing … remember … open and honest discussion with mutual respect."

***

What Fred thought would take an hour or so turned into a three-hour exercise as each group debated, argued, and debated some more about what they thought their measurements for their strategic business unit should be. Fred, Narvell, and Chris rotated groups just about every hour when Fred realized that this wasn't going to be a quick session. By rotating, each of the three men got to hear what everyone in the room was thinking.

As Narvell arrived at his third group of the day, the admin and support managers, he noticed something that made him realize this may not be going as well as he had hoped. As he sat and listened, Narvell realized that the younger, and/or newer managers in the group were doing the majority of the talking. One of them would explain what they thought the metrics should be. Then the entire group would discuss the ideas. What Narvell saw was less than half of the "old timers," regardless of their actual age, presenting any ideas. However, these were the same people who were the first to say what was wrong with each metric presented. As Narvell thought back on the other two groups, he recognized the same thing was happening in those conversations as well.

Before he became too discouraged, Narvell looked around the room and saw some very big exceptions to what he thought was happening. He saw Allyson over with the sales and marketing group actually leading the conversation and encouraging her managers to speak up; good or bad, she wanted to hear their thoughts. And thinking back on the engineers, he did allow himself to acknowledge that Jimbo was trying his best to drag an idea or two out of everyone on his team. Realizing that it wasn't as bad as he had just thought, Narvell smiled slightly and then let himself become engrossed in the conversation of the admin and support managers.

Shortly after 3:00 p.m., Fred asked everyone to come back together. There was obvious anticipation on the faces and in the voices of those in the room. As everyone settled back into their seats waiting to hear what Fred was going to say and do next, they had one last surprise coming from their CEO. Standing in front of them now, Fred looked around the room smiling. After he had taken a long hard look at each person, Fred glanced back at Narvell and Chris before he spoke. "To each of you that just gave up the vast majority of your day, I say thank you. The board says thank you. I think what we have done here today is a great start. Do we have a long way to go? Yes. Do we have a lot of roadblocks to overcome? Yes. Do I think we can do it? Yes. Originally, I thought we'd now discuss the measurements each group selected. But I've been thinking about what all Narvell, Chris, and Max have said today. Somewhere during the past three-plus hours, I figured out that that's not the way to do it. I wasn't listening to what these young men told us. We don't need to be trying to agree upon the metrics you all just hammered out. No, we don't. Your teams do.

"So, we're going to call it a day. I want you all to get together with your next level supervisors and their teams, along with your staffs, and let them try and shoot holes in your measurements. After everyone is satisfied with these metrics, then you can start working on theirs. After you've got theirs in place, go down another level. Take it all the way down. I suspect that Rob and Allyson will have a bit of a jump on the rest of us, but don't give up and don't get frustrated. Narvell, you and Chris can help Jimbo in Engineering. I'll see if Matt and I can handle the admin and support teams. Any last questions?"

Jimbo spoke up very quickly. "Fred, what happens when we run head long into the human roadblock? I'm not going to pretend that we're not going to struggle mightily in Engineering with this."

"Jimbo, if the only team you get engaged in Engineering is your own, we'll take it. Don't threaten or force anyone. Let's take what we can get and use those pockets of interest as examples. If/when we get success stories out of these willing participants, then we can start applying a little pressure to others. Hopefully, when we get there, peer pressure will become a big advocate for change. You good with that idea, Jimbo?"

"Yes, sir. That takes a bit of the pressure off of me anyway when you look at the big picture. I think I still need to talk to you a bit though about the elephant that left the room." When Jimbo said this, the entire room laughed. There definitely was a change of attitude from the morning session when Narvell and Chris had been presenting.

"All right then. I'll let you all get back to your offices and at least check some e-mail, and fight a fire or two, before you go home. Narvell, Chris, on behalf of M.E. Burdette Company … thank you."

***

Narvell and Chris had packed up their computers and notepads and had fully expected to debrief with Fred after everyone had left. But Fred had an entirely different idea. He told the two men to go on home and decompress. He wanted them to think about the day and what, if anything, they had learned through the various conversations both in the morning when they had presented and in the session following when the teams were working on their strategic business unit measurements.

When Narvell got home, all he really wanted to do was sit down and *not* think. His head hurt from all the various conversations he had listened to and tried to interpret with regard to the intent of the speaker. Were they for this grand idea or against? Were they actually offering up ideas, or trying to snowball the others on the team? He opened the door and headed inside, dropping his computer bag on the couch. After going into the kitchen and finding a beer in the refrigerator, Narvell opened the bottle and made his way to the sofa. Sitting down, he sipped on the beer as he tried to replay the entire day in order. Thinking back through the morning presentations that Chris and he had given was the easy part. The more Narvell thought about what they had said and how they had said it, the better he was feeling. And thinking about Max and the story of the tape measure, Narvell was certain that they had gotten it right in having Max tell the story himself. It was the brainstorming session that Narvell kept getting stuck on.

Just as Narvell was standing up to go get another beer, the doorbell rang. Changing direction midstep, Narvell walked to the front door and opened it. As soon as the door was open far enough, Annie burst through the doorway and hugged Narvell around the neck. For a long time. For a very long time. She didn't say anything. She just hugged him. Almost to the point that he couldn't breathe. Finally, Annie began to laugh and let go of Narvell just long enough so he could catch his breath. She then hugged him again.

"Narvie, you did it. I really think you did it. Both Allyson and Rob stopped by to talk to me after your meeting. They couldn't say enough nice things about you and Chris. I don't think Allyson's totally convinced yet that this will help the bottom line, but she definitely believes that what Rob is doing can be used to improve the top line significantly. Narvell … I am … so proud of you." And then Annie Gerdes kissed Narvell. And it was not a friendly congratulatory type kiss. No, this was a passionate kiss that conveyed her feelings very clearly.

When the two of them finally separated, Narvell looked at Annie. "Wow. I'd thank you, but that seems a bit cheesy considering that kiss. But … I do want to do the gentlemanly thing and ask you to dinner. How about tomorrow night?"

"Mr. Mann, I'd love to."

"Great! I would've said tonight, but Chris is going to come over later to compare notes. And I want to get all of my thoughts into our blog before he gets here. You are more than welcome to stay and listen. We'll probably order a pizza or something for dinner."

"Sure. I'd like that, Narvell. Will you at least get me a beer before you start blogging?" Annie replied with a smile.

Narvell smiled back and went into the kitchen where he opened the last beer in the refrigerator. Walking back into the living room, he handed the beer to Annie and smiled. "I'm going to go blog for a while. Do you mind texting Chris and asking him to pick up some soda or beer on his way? That beer in your hand is the last thing to drink in the entire house, except for water."

"Not a problem," Annie responded pulling out her cell phone.

Narvell then turned, grabbed his computer bag, and headed back into his bedroom. Pulling out his laptop, he quickly plugged in the power cord and turned the computer on. As soon as he had a network connection established, Narvell navigated his way to the blog and began typing. When he had finished, he read over his blog entry twice to make sure he hadn't forgotten anything.

Presenting our Case for Measuring Success

Posted on **October 10, 2011**
Reply

Wow. What a day! I had no idea that our presentation would go so well. From what I can tell, there are plenty of managers at M.E. Burdette Co. that want things to change. They really are interested in the company's success. The day got off a bit rocky with Bill Cooke and Bryan Steinman. But after they left, things seemed to calm down some.

I'm still not sure though about who is on board and who isn't. The biggest thing I' noticed when we split up into teams was how the "old guard" acted. With a few notable exceptions, the rest seemed to sit back and not contribute much. But, boy were they ready to pounce on othersideas. As soon as the newer managers floated out ideas, many of the old guard would tear them down, telling us why the metric wouldn't work. From where I was sitting it appeared that about 50 or 60% of the "old guard" fell into that category. I need to remember to talk to Fred *AND* Max about that. Is this common when trying to make change happen?

Overall, I must say that the top down support is REALLY, REALLY there. Fred has done a phenomenal job championing the concept of the tape measure. And when we left today, he clearly left it in the management team's lap to continue pushing it down. The big challenge will be to make sure it gets down to the bottom and that our employees at the lowest levels take ownership in all of this and start driving it all back up.

I can't wait to see what this new process of measuring for success brings us!!!!

Posted in Blogs from the book | Leave a reply

Chapter 18

It Does *Not* Happen Overnight

October 11

The rest of the week was a blur of activity around M.E. Burdette Co. Fred and Matt spent half of each day discussing the new measurement methodology and looking for a few willing participants to pilot the system for them. Chris probably had the easiest task. He was riding shotgun with Rob Allison, and Allison was proving to be a huge champion for them. Rob quickly found eager participants in the Southeast and Southwest sales regions, and Annie's boss George had found Allyson right after the meeting Monday afternoon and told her that Marketing was on board. It was Narvell and Jimbo, working on Engineering, who ran into the biggest roadblocks. It seemed as though each and every person in the Engineering department was working behind the scenes to make it as hard as possible on the two men.

After Fred had explained to Narvell and Jimbo that Bill Cooke would be on vacation for the next five weeks, Narvell thought that perhaps it wouldn't be so difficult to change the way things were measured in Engineering. Boy, was he ever wrong. Everyone in the engineering office knew the situation: Bill was on a forced vacation and then would meet with Fred before his possible return to work. While several of the engineers had approached Jimbo to give him their support, each of the ones that had come forward did it in an almost secret fashion. They had either come in early before anyone else was in the office, or they had stayed late. Since Jimbo had been the first one in the office every morning for years and quite often stayed late, it was relatively easy to catch him when no one else was around.

Narvell couldn't even convince the other members of the engineering support team to participate. After three full days of no progress, Narvell and Jimbo resigned themselves to the fact that the only manager in Engineering willing to try this new way of measuring success was Jimbo. So the die was cast. Narvell would only be working with Jimbo's product team—one product family team out of four. There was just no interest from the research and development team, the manufacturing engineering team, the industrial engineering team, or even from the engineering support team. Narvell and Jimbo had only been able to convince (actually, tell) one team out of seven to participate in this pilot project measuring success. By the end of the week, it was obvious to Narvell that something wasn't right. Even the five engineers that reported directly to Jimbo were not really interested in participating. It was as though they all wished that Narvell and Jimbo would just go on and fail so things could get back to normal.

Even though Fred and Chris were having some early success with their work, Narvell was feeling like this might just be a big waste of time. The only thing that was going right for Narvell was Annie. The two of them had spent Tuesday and Wednesday evenings together—alone, and, not a single word about work either night. After not seeing Annie on Thursday at all, Narvell had decided that he wanted to see a lot more of Annie Gerdes.

***

Over the next five weeks, Fred personally met with Narvell and each of the pilot teams. Chris had slowly reduced his hours at M.E. Burdette Co. and had returned to the family business, checking in formally with Fred and Narvell weekly, and informally with Narvell almost every single day. As the holidays were approaching, the mood around M.E. Burdette Co. was improving greatly. Fred and Matt both felt that when they got the month-end figures for November they would see progress with the Administrative Services Division. Narvell had been meeting with Allyson and George at least twice each week in addition to the time that Fred and Narvell were with them. Allyson had reported that the two sales regions that were piloting the measurement system had simply decided to do exactly what Rob was doing in the Northeast region. This made it all very simple. And the numbers supported it.

Big Week – Big Problem

Posted on **October 14, 2011**
Reply

>   The first week of trying to correct what is wrong has come to a close. Our CEO, Fred Schmidt, along with his CFO Matt Ward, have made significant strides in the Administrative Services Division…. primarily, in my opinion, because they carry a big stick. They've gotten four different departments/teams to pilot for them. It's always good to have champions like the C.O. level guys pushing the agenda.
>
>   Chris has definitely been living on easy street working with Sales and Marketing. After Allyson appeared to me as a huge opponent when she was attacking our presentation, she has turned into the biggest proponent you could imagine. She and George from Marketing are so on board that it appears as though they might force everyone under them to play. I know that Fred talked to her Wednesday evening and emphasized the need to NOT mandate. *There must be buy-in at the lower levels.*
>
>   As for Jimbo and me, I really think we are missing something! It should not be this hard. How is it that you can get people to privately say they support what you are doing, but not ever get on the bus with you? What is going on in Engineering? We've got to figure this one out, if we are going to move forward……..

Posted in Blogs from the book | Leave a reply

Fred sat down with Narvell and Chris the week of Thanksgiving to discuss what the next steps were if the pilot areas showed strong improvement at the end of November. He was surprised when Chris showed up in his office with Max. "Max, I didn't expect to be seeing you today. Come on in," Fred said, extending a hand to shake the hand of the man whose philosophy might just be what M.E. Burdette Co. needed to stay in business.

"Fred, it's good to see you. I thought I'd come listen in on the progress you all have made since the first of October."

As the men sat down in the informal seating area in Fred's office, Narvell wasted no time in getting to the point. "Max, Fred and Matt have gotten some pretty good buy-in from the admin services people. We expect to show some significant progress with the pilot areas there."

Fred interrupted before Narvell could continue. "Actually, I suspect that we got the cooperation because the two of us told a couple of teams that they were going to do it. I'm not sure whether or not they are willing participants at this point." Fred finished his statement with a hearty laugh that everyone joined in on.

"I understand completely, Fred," Max said. "Sometimes you have to use your position to emphasize your dedication to a decision. And in return, the employees respond. Not always in a willing way initially. But in the end if their jobs get easier and they see the big picture, they'll become converts. Please, Narvell. Continue. I'm afraid we interrupted you."

"Not a problem, Max. The sales and marketing pilots are going extremely well. Rob Allison and Chris have done a phenomenal job working with Allyson, George, and their teams. It probably doesn't hurt that George has Annie as a cheerleader on all of this. She really talked it up with her coworkers. We should have updated weekly reports from the sales regions by the end of the day. The sales teams are reporting everything to Allyson weekly. George and his team in Marketing are on a monthly reporting cycle to Allyson, even though they update weekly as well."

"Why is that, Narvell? Chris?" Max asked, looking at each of the two young men.

Chris answered. "George and his team asked how they would be reporting if this system went companywide. We explained that at the top levels of the company, most of the numbers would be reported monthly and/or quarterly. Their response to this was that they wanted to measure weekly or by project and then report up to Allyson monthly. By the way, she very quickly agreed, which created instant buy-in on the part of quite a few of George's employees."

"Excellent work. It sounds like you've got quite a few good people at the top, Fred," Max said, looking across the coffee table at Fred.

"I wish it was all good news, Max," Narvell stated in a serious tone as he dialed in on the most difficult part of their journey. "I feel like we are failing in Engineering."

"Why is that? Aren't you getting any improvements there?"

"Well sir, yes … some …. But at the same time, Jimbo and I feel like we're beating our heads against the wall most of the time. It's like we're missing something. I'm not sure what it is, but it just doesn't feel right. The only team participating as a pilot is Jimbo's product team. And to a man, they seem very skeptical," Narvell said and shook his head showing his frustration. This was the area he had been given to work on and it was doing the worst.

"Narvell, trust your instincts," Max said, leaning forward in his seat to emphasize what he was saying to Narvell. "What does Jimbo think? Does he think something's wrong as well?"

"Yes, sir. We've discussed it almost every day. On numerous occasions, Jimbo has had employees in Engineering, some who have over twenty years with the company, come to him privately telling him they like what we're doing. But … they won't do anything to help. They won't speak up in the meetings we've had. It's as if they're afraid of something. But Bill isn't here intimidating anyone. So … what's the problem?"

"Maybe that is the problem," Max interjected. "Fred, when is Bill coming back to work?"

"He's supposed to come back next Monday."

"Then I suspect you need to have a conversation with some employees before then," Max said to Fred before turning towards Narvell. "Son, do you remember my four guiding principles I discussed when I told the tape measure story?"

"Of course. I've heard it from you, Chris, and Tom: One, find your tape measure; two, you've got to have high personal ethics to guide you; three, treat everyone with respect; and four, if you fail at any of these guidelines, you won't be an employee at the end of the day," Narvell repeated for Max with a smile on his face.

"Excellent. Fred, I'm not going to tell you how to run your company. But, it may be time to think about numbers two through four in regards to Bill Cooke," Max said as he stood up. "I've got a meeting downtown. Sorry I can't stay longer. Fred, don't hesitate to call if you need anything."

Fred stood and shook Max's hand before he left, and then turned back to Narvell and Chris. "So do you both think Bill is the problem?"

Narvell looked at Chris before answering. "Fred … honestly I'm not sure. I can't believe that one person could have that much influence when they're not even there. He may be part of the problem but not all of it. It just doesn't seem that it's all Bill."

"Okay. I'll call a couple of engineering employees in that I know best and see what I can get out of them. And just so you and Jimbo know, Narvell, Bill is supposed to report to me first thing Monday. He is not to go to his office. I told him that before he could return, we would have to have a very serious conversation about his actions. Thanks, guys. Let me know if you find out anything else," Fred said and then stood up to signal the end of the meeting.

Narvell and Chris headed back towards Engineering to fill Jimbo in on the meeting. As they turned the corner just outside the engineering offices, Chris ran into Bryan Steinman who was looking at the floor and talking on his cell phone. Chris bumped the older engineer so hard he dropped his phone. Bending over to pick it up, Bryan muttered loud enough for both of the other men to hear. "Why don't you two get the hell out of here? By the end of next week, things will be back to normal and your little game will be over."

The Good, the Bad & the Ugly?

Posted on **November 21, 2011**
Reply

The Good:

OUTSIDE SALES – SOUTHEAST REGION

UOM	BASELINE	PREVIOUS	% CHANGE	CURRENT	% CHANGE
Sales Dollars (Wkly)	115,700	112,652	2.63%↓	121,333	7.71%↑
Gross Margin	29.7%	32.05%	7.91%↑	34.80%	9.26%↑
Cost of Sales	34.10%	35.90%	5.28%↑	33.90%	5.87%↓

OUTSIDE SALES – SOUTHWEST REGION

UOM	BASELINE	PREVIOUS	% CHANGE	CURRENT	% CHANGE
Sales Dollars (Wkly)	124,898	138,002	10.49%↑	152,775	10.70%↑
Gross Margin	26.80%	29.80%	11.19%↑	32.60%	10.45%↑
Cost of Sales	48.50%	42.05%	13.30%↓	40.10%	4.02%↓

The Southeast Region is making good progress, but the Southwest Region is knocking the lights out of the place. Take a look at those numbers. Just like we were taught in school. If you measure something and people are involved, make sure they see the results. Just by making the metrics visible, you can get as much as 10% improvement without doing anything else. Here's the proof.

The Bad:

We're still getting no buy-in from Engineering. Fred is going to have a heart-to-heart with Bill before he can come back to work. But, I just can't believe that he has this much influence on everyone when he's not even here. We need to crack the code on how to get Engineering on board.

The Ugly?

Bryan Steinman. Chris and I talked to Jimbo about Bryan and his attitude. Maybe he is the negative influence we are experiencing. But how could he have so much power when all he does is manage a small team in R&D?????

Posted in Blogs from the book | Leave a reply

Chris started to say something in return, but Narvell grabbed him by the arm and nearly pulled him off his feet as he quickly headed towards Jimbo's office. As they walked in, Jimbo was just hanging up the phone. Narvell looked at Jimbo and didn't try to hide the concerned look on his face. "Jimbo, we need to talk …"

***

Narvell read through his latest blog entry and then turned off the computer and climbed into bed. The last few weeks had been extremely hard on the young man as he tried to balance a now promising career with a social life. He had been out with Annie every free evening he'd had since that first date, so coming home this evening and doing nothing more than watching television was a welcome change. After the ten o'clock news, he had turned off the television and blogged about his journey. He had received the sales numbers from Rob by e-mail just before he left the office and hadn't even looked at them until he opened his blog.

He was asleep before his head hit the pillow. Narvell was dead to the world as he slept. But a restful night it was not to be. Narvell dreamed about the interaction with Bryan earlier in the day. He replayed in his dreams the words Max had said to Fred. And he dreamed about Bill coming back the next Monday and firing him for a second time. It was not a restful night for Narvell.

But while Narvell was sleeping, his roommate was just starting his work. Bobby Evans had come home around eight o'clock and chatted with Narvell about Annie and work. When Narvell told him about the rather rude exchange with Bryan, Bobby took note. He had already heard the tales of Bill Cooke and his desire to keep a firm grip on the Engineering department. So when Narvell recounted what had happened in the hall and talked about the sheer cockiness in Bryan's voice, Bobby began to process the entire scenario.

After Narvell had gone to bed, Bobby made a couple of phone calls and then went to his room. Turning on the computer that was rarely used for anything more than checking e-mail, Bobby began to surf the Internet. Taking notes from time to time, Bobby continued his search until the early hours of the morning. When Narvell woke Tuesday morning, Bobby had only been in bed for two hours. Bobby had left the notes from his Internet research on the kitchen table with a note to Narvell explaining what he had found. The problem was Narvell never went into the kitchen Tuesday morning. When he emerged from his bedroom, Narvell was already running late, and so he left for the office without his morning cup of coffee.

As Narvell walked into the engineering offices that morning, he saw Jimbo waving at him from across the room. Seeing the excitement on Jimbo's face, Narvell didn't even bother stopping by his cubicle to take off his coat or check his e-mail. He went straight across the room to Jimbo's small, yet functional, office. Stepping inside the door, he found Jimbo seated at his desk and Paula, Bill Cooke's administrative assistant, seated in the lone side chair.

"Narvell, would you mind closing the door?" Jimbo asked in an unusually soft voice.

"Sure thing. What's up?"

"Paula, would you mind repeating what you just told me?" Jimbo said looking over at the middle-aged woman seated across the desk from him.

"Not a problem, Jimbo. It's not like I expect to have a job at the end of the day anyway. As I said, I think I know why you two aren't getting any cooperation from the staff. I believe that they're being intimidated, and from what I've seen over the past four or five weeks, it's working. The problem is I don't know how you could ever prove anything," Paula stated, glancing back and forth between Jimbo and Narvell.

"Well, who do you think is doing it, Paula?" Narvell asked politely, trying to hide the excitement that was starting to well up inside him. Finally, a clue, Narvell thought to himself before Paula could answer his question.

"First, let me say that I don't think Bill is doing any of it. Don't get me wrong. If he was here, I'm sure he would condone it and would most likely be as big a roadblock as any of the others. From what I've heard, it all starts with Bryan. He's got something going on on the side. I'm not sure what it is. But, I've seen him meet with each and every person in Engineering within an hour after the two of you do. You might say I've had plenty of idle time on my hands since Bill was put out on his hiatus."

"Why now, Paula?" Jimbo asked. "Why are you coming to us now? Why not last week or the week before last? Something's happened, hasn't it?"

"Yes. Bryan came by my desk yesterday evening, as I was getting ready to leave. He threatened me. He said that if I said anything to you two, he would make sure that I was out the door on Bill's first day back. You know, I've only got a couple more years before I can retire, and I don't want to lose it all now. But … I refuse to be threatened. I didn't even know what he was talking about … which doesn't really matter …. I will not be intimidated. I wasn't raised that way. I've worked here for over thirty years. I started when I graduated from college. Tough job market, so I took the first job that was offered. I've been here ever since. Jimbo, I don't want to leave yet … but … I don't … know what to do. All I know is that you should do the right thing and be dedicated to those who respect you. Well, it's obvious that Bryan doesn't respect me … and honestly … I don't think Bill … has the guts … to stand up to him."

As Paula finished her statement, she broke down and sobbed. Jimbo stood up from his chair and motioned Narvell to close the blinds on the window next to his door. Then he bent down and hugged Paula but said nothing for the longest time. When she had calmed down a bit, Jimbo straightened back up and looked her in the eyes. "Paula, you are not going anywhere. We're working with Fred to figure out what is going on here, and you have just given us the first solid piece of evidence. I'll talk to Fred myself, okay?"

"Thank you, Jimbo, Narvell. I truly do appreciate you two and hope beyond hope that you find what's wrong here. Sorry about the tears. I need to go and fix my face. I must be a mess," Paula responded as she stood to leave. Before Narvell could open the door for her, Paula reached over, squeezed his hand and mouthed the words "Thank you."

Jimbo and Narvell spent the next two hours going over all of the notes they had collected while trying to find engineering teams to pilot the new measurement system. They couldn't find anything from any of the meetings that added to what Paula had told them. So, with a frustrated sound in his voice, Jimbo resigned himself to the next step. "Well, Narvell, I guess we might as well fill in Fred on what happened this morning. Drop off your coat and meet me in Fred's office."

Coming out of Jimbo's office, Jimbo turned right and Narvell went left to stop by his cubicle. As he walked down the long corridor of cubicles, he noticed that quite a few engineers were staring at him. He couldn't worry about the reason for that right now. Stepping into his cubicle, Narvell dropped his coat over the desk chair and started to turn around when he remembered his cell phone. Reaching into his coat pocket he grabbed the phone, punched the button on top to check for messages, and headed out of Engineering.

Narvell had one message on his phone. It was from Bobby of all people. Why would he be texting me? Narvell thought to himself as he navigated to the message. What he saw in the message made absolutely no sense at all.

Narv—you didn't see the stuff I left in the kitchen, did you? 1 question: what does ZL&S mfg engineers have to do with your co.?

***

After Jimbo had explained the conversation between Paula, Narvell, and himself, Jimbo then repeated what the two of them knew, or more appropriately didn't know, about what was going on. Fred interrupted Jimbo at that point. "Guys, I need to bring you up to speed on the Bill situation. I just left HR. We terminated Bill this morning. Actually, we allowed him to resign. It was easier than fighting about it with him. I met with him last night. He refused to back off of his position. He continually came back to his statement that Narvell didn't have a clue, and that what we are trying to do would ruin the company. I finally got tired of listening to him and asked point blank, 'Will you be on board when you return Monday and help us with the new measurement system?' I couldn't believe his response. He said 'No' without even hesitating. He left me no choice. What Max told us about his philosophy towards culture rang very loud and true in my ears when Bill said 'No.' It's time we started treating everyone with mutual respect. It sounds like we may have a lot of training to do in Engineering to get them on the same page as us."

Narvell looked at Jimbo and then Fred before speaking. "What does this mean for Paula? She came about as close as anyone to telling us what is going on."

Fred's response put both of the younger men at ease. "Paula's not going anywhere. She's been a great employee for us for thirty-plus years. I'll find her a place with the same or better pay. We don't want to lose her, and not just because she's a good hand. She may know a bit more about the issues in Engineering."

That's when Bobby's text message popped back into Narvell's head. "Fred, Jimbo, what do either of you know about Z.L.&S. Manufacturing Engineers?" Narvell asked, hoping this wasn't a bunch of day-dreaming on Bobby's part.

Jimbo responded without even thinking about it. "Z.L.&S. Manufacturing Engineers Inc. is the company that we farm product maintenance out to when we have too many projects on our plates. Why?"

"Apparently my roommate, who has quite a financial mind but no drive or desire, found something on Z.L.&S. that he thought we'd be interested in."

"Well, what did he tell you, Narvell?" Jimbo prodded.

"That's it so far. He just asked what they have to do with our company. He said he left me some stuff at the house."

"Can you call him?" Fred said.

"Sure thing. Hang on," Narvell replied, pulling his phone from his pocket.

Narvell sat and listened to Bobby rant and rave about how good he was for a full five minutes before he ever spoke about what he had found. When he finally finished telling Narvell everything he had found, he wrapped up the conversation with his usual accusatory bravado. "I told you that Bill Cooke fella was stealing from the company. Now, all you've got to do is connect the dots. Thank you very much! Sorry I can't talk longer. It's my last class before the Thanksgiving break. See ya, Narv." And with that, the line went dead.

Narvell looked across at Fred and Jimbo. His face had turned somewhat ashen as Bobby had been talking. Now he was about to explain what his up-until-this-point goofy and drunk roommate had found. "Gentlemen, I think Bobby may have found something. Does the name Jeff Long mean anything to either of you?"

"Yeah." Jimbo said. "Jeff retired about four years ago. He'd been an engineer for us for over twenty years. Why?"

"Hang on. How about Mike Zinn?" Narvell continued.

Jimbo shook his head no. But when Narvell looked over at Fred, he saw an expression that truly worried him. A scowl had come across Fred's face, and it was clear that he was trying to choose what he said next very carefully. "Narvell … what does this have to do with the topic?" Fred finally asked, already knowing what answer Narvell was going give.

"L is for Long. Z is for Zinn."

"Yes," Fred said, now shaking his head. "I know Mike Zinn. He's my ex-brother-in-law and best friends with one of our board members, J.P. Lewis. That's who vouched for the firm when they bid on our outsourced work. It had to come to the board due to a budget freeze during the last recession. Where is this going, Narvell …?"

"Well sir, guess what the S stands for?"

Both of the other men stared at each other before Fred motioned for Narvell to continue.

"Steinman. As in Bryan Steinman." Narvell said with a big smile on his face.

Chapter 19

The Journey Continues

January 3

The manufacturing floor had been shut down for scheduled maintenance the previous week, providing an extended holiday for production employees. This had caused all kinds of problems, both real and imagined, for the sales force nationwide, and the sales teams' problems had landed in the middle of the engineering offices on January 3rd. With the holidays behind them, and a new year of much needed hope in front of them, Fred had gathered his team back together to discuss their expectations of the results to be posted for each of the pilot areas at the end of the week. Fred had intentionally called this meeting for late in the day to allow Jimbo and the engineering team time to provide initial responses to most of the issues they found from both Sales and Manufacturing this morning when the manufacturing floor started production again.

Already seated around the conference table in Fred's office were Fred, Jimbo, Allyson, Rob, and Matt. Fred had asked Max if he could join them. But Max had politely declined, saying he thought the progress over the past six weeks was tremendous and that he didn't see that he could add anything new or different to the discussion. Narvell and Chris walked into the office and took their seats in the middle of Fred's explanation to Allyson and Rob about the management changes in Engineering.

"As I was saying, Rob, and I may paraphrase it just a bit, but Bill essentially fired himself. He refused to get on the bus with us. He was not about to change the way he ran Engineering." Fred explained.

Rob nodded, paused, and then asked, "But was he, or wasn't he involved in the … what do I call it … scandal?"

"You can call it what you want. I call it embezzlement. And no, we don't think at this point Bill actually did anything illegal. Maybe a paid golf outing or two with Jeff Long or Mike Zinn. Probably quite a few times with Bryan; they had a social relationship. I know that. But, I don't know how often Bryan paid versus Bill. We'll let the District Attorney sort all that out. We've got bigger things to think about."

Rob just wouldn't let the subject drop. The more he heard, the more interesting it became. "Look, if you all don't mind, I've been back in my region five of the last six weeks, so I've missed out on all of this. And I guess the only thing I'm asking for is to understand what happened. Just tell me to shut up, or tell me what I can't talk about outside of this room. It's just that I keep getting asked by my employees and the other regional managers."

And since no one said anything, Rob continued his questioning. "So, Bill just didn't want to change. Okay. I get that. But how did you figure out what Bryan was doing? Did Bill tell you?"

Fred looked at Narvell and nodded as if to say *explain*.

Narvell wasn't sure where to start, so he went all the way back to the beginning. "My roommate heard Chris, Annie, and me talking about what was going on back in September. When he heard me talking about Bill and his management style, he immediately decided that Bill was stealing from the company. The longer it went on and the more we talked about it when we were at our house, the more convinced Bobby was that Bill was up to something. He's still in college and he had plenty of free time, not to mention quite an imagination, so he started searching the Internet for Bill's name. Of course, he really wasn't hitting on anything important, but it didn't stop him from looking. He said that his dad taught him that most people who come into money improperly usually don't do a very good job of hiding it, actually just the opposite … they blow it on all kinds of stupid stuff that leaves a trail. So he went looking. Problem was he couldn't find anything on Bill.

"Then one night he heard us talking about Bryan, and his threats about how everything would be normal when Bill got back and that Jimbo and I would be gone. So off Bobby went again, and this time he got a hit. Using Bryan's name, the state and town he got a hit on a business filing at the state capitol. Bryan was listed as the registered agent for Z.L.&S. Manufacturing Engineers Inc. when it was incorporated. He pulled the paperwork up, and the officers and shareholders of record were listed as Mike Zinn, Jeff Long, and Bryan Steinman. He kept digging and found out that all three live right here in town. He even knew that Mike was Fred's brother-in-law at one time."

Rob was clearly impressed with the story, but before he could ask any more questions, Fred looked over at Narvell. "Son, don't stop there. Tell Rob the rest of the story. You and Jimbo get all of the credit for cleaning house."

Narvell's smile couldn't get any bigger as he launched into the final piece of the puzzle. "When Jimbo heard about it, he about came unglued. I believe your words were *'So that explains why Bryan's team never had to take on any other assignments. They already had other work. Our work … on the outside.'* And really, without missing a beat, Jimbo suggested to Fred that we have security escort Bryan out of the building in the middle of the day in front of everyone. If you're going to make a statement, do it in a big way, right? And, boy, was that big. Fred had Bryan's entire team cut off from the computer network at the same time. When Bryan was screaming at the help desk to fix a problem, security walked in and escorted him to HR, and then the parking lot. They were actually working on outsourced projects on our own computers.

"Once that happened, Bryan's three team members panicked. But before any of them could say or do anything, Jimbo had people streaming into his office telling him what was going on and explaining the way Bryan and his guys had been threatening and coercing employees into keeping quiet. And I must say that Jimbo handled it all very professionally. He refused to condemn without an investigation. Taking copious notes on the whole matter, and promising that the company would fix everything very quickly."

Fred then decided he had better wrap up this story, so he interrupted Narvell at that point. "And to calm everyone's fears, we moved Jimbo into Bill's office as interim director. And I'm proud to announce that the interim label came off this morning. Congratulations, Jimbo."

"Thank you, Fred. I appreciate the vote of confidence. Now, can we get on with the meeting? You guys may like talking about this topic, but it makes me a bit uneasy. You know what I mean? I worked with each of those guys for years. I'd rather just move on and not talk about it. Not forget it, ever … just not talk about it, okay?" Jimbo said shaking Fred's outstretched hand.

As Fred released Jimbo's hand, he nodded slightly before speaking. "You're right Jimbo. I'm sorry. We should've taken it offline when we were done. Rob, no more questions right now, okay? Now, the reason we're here. What are our expectations for the results we should have posted this week? We've already seen about half of November and we definitely saw some things happen. Not big by any means but enough to be encouraged. And seeing some of the sales regions' weekly numbers, there is definitely something to be said for all the sales teams being measured the same way *and* at a very basic team level. Definitely good news there. Allyson, what do you and Rob think?"

"You know that I signed on in a big way and supported what Rob was doing when you asked for pilot areas, Fred. I'm glad I did. I probably should have been listening to Rob from the beginning. I tried to get him to do what everyone else was doing when he hired on. Now, I'm glad he asked to let him measure things his way. That was a big gamble, Rob. You asked for six months to prove you could do it in a different way and you did. Your track record is what sold me on this as much as what Narvell and Chris presented. And our regions that are piloting it are making good steady progress, six weeks in. They're not going to be overtaking Rob's team anytime soon, but give 'em a year and look out." Allyson finished by giving Rob a smile and a quick wink.

"Couldn't have said it better myself, Allyson," was all Rob could add to the conversation at that point.

Fred continued around the table. "Matt, what do you have to say about our admin services?"

"Honestly Fred, I feel a bit like a failure on this one. We've made virtually no progress since we set the metrics up on our pilot areas. When you stepped out to start talking to the nonpilot managers about what was happening, we kinda lost our steam. And then I must admit that I turned my attention to the engineering dollars. Jimbo, if you all can really handle that same number of outsourced projects internally, you'll save the company somewhere north of $500,000 a year."

Jimbo leaned forward in his chair so Matt could see his face as he spoke. "Matt, those guys were already doing the work on our time. They had exactly one outside engineer working on this stuff. I might need to hire one entry level engineer to make it all work but we should have no problem at all doing it."

"All right. I believe you. Then at least the time I spent chasing invoices and project numbers for you will pay off in some way. Fred, I can't add much more than that."

Fred spoke softly now as he addressed Matt's remarks. "No. That's perfectly all right. It's a team effort, and I didn't expect us all to hit home runs on our first at bat. Jimbo, what about you and Narvell with Engineering? Anything new?"

"As I told Matt," Jimbo immediately jumped in, "we can definitely handle the outsourced work with maybe one more body. That's big to the bottom line. But more importantly, we've had every team in the department step forward now and ask to change the way we measure things. I've actually said no. I want everyone in Engineering to see what my team's numbers look like first and to see what the other pilot areas look like before we make across the board changes. I don't know that I could handle the chaos if we tried to change everything at once."

Narvell picked up at the point that Jimbo's voice trailed off. "To be fair to Jimbo …. We had a department meeting and discussed the entire situation. None of us wanted it to look like Jimbo was just trying to add feathers to his cap since his team was the only pilot in the department. And I will tell you that almost everyone in the room voiced their support for what Jimbo is trying to do. There were a few stick-in-the-muds who are definitely old guard, but if everything else we've learned from Max, Tom, and Chris is correct, those few dissidents will find a new home somewhere else before too long. Oh … by the way. I'll brag on Jimbo. His numbers when posted tomorrow will look pretty darn good for one month out."

Fred brought the conversation full circle. "Before we close, Narvell, do you or Chris have anything else to add?"

Chris, who had been unusually quiet throughout the entire conversation, spoke up. "Well, yes. Yes, I do. I'm going to be the glass-is-half-empty guy today. I know it sounds like things are going pretty well. But that's because you are dealing with the willing participants at this point. I suspect that overall the numbers will be good as they're posted over the next couple of days. But, remember what Matt said about struggling. As you add additional departments and teams to the mix, you will struggle—mightily at times. Sometimes, you'll find simple solutions, other times you may have to start over in an area. Please remember that. Housholder Sprockets and our measurement system weren't created in day, or a week, or a month, or a quarter. It wasn't even created in a year. It took us years and lots of hard work to get where we are today. I suspect it will take M.E. Burdette a while to get it right. But … don't give up. It's not about quick incremental success. It's about getting it right in the long haul. You guys have got a great team, just keep doing what you're doing and you'll get there. And remember, perhaps the most important thing of all, it's never over. This is part of what continuous improvement is all about. Narvell, you need to go put that speech I just made in your blog. That was good stuff."

Everyone in the room had a good laugh at Chris' closing comment. As they were breaking up the session, Fred looked over at Narvell. "Narvell … I know Chris was kidding with you, but if you haven't already put anything in that blog of yours about success in the long haul and continuous improvement, you need to. You also need to make sure that we have a copy of your blog as a guide to keep us on the road to success and a history of where we came from. Okay?"

***

"I'm telling you the truth Annie. Fred told me to blog about Chris' closing comments this morning. So I did. And then I thought that since this was turning into a historical record of the thoughts, pain, and successes that we experienced, we probably needed to acknowledge the fact that my own, slightly deranged roommate, actually played a pretty big role in breaking the code in Engineering. I don't know how long it would have taken had he not found that information on Bryan."

It's Continuous Improvement

Posted on **January 3, 2012**
Reply

And don't forget it!!!

This journey can be, and most certainly is, a long and rough road. It's not about quick incremental changes and short term success. It is all about the long haul. You must be prepared to make very small changes at times. You might only be able to convince a very small group, at first, of the need to change and measure the right things.

It starts with helping those who want to succeed find their tape measure. These believers must understand their place in the organization and how they fit into the big picture. Then they must measure those few things that truly are important and show success. Take whatever success you get and build from there.

REMEMBER…….. The organization didn't get where it is today overnight. And you are not going to change it overnight. Accept the fact that it is a journey and embrace it.

Another thing: Look for those individuals like my roommate Bobby. The ones that think outside the box. They might appear on the surface to be a bit off-center, but listening to what they have to say invites ownership on the part of all employees. AND occasionally you find a real gem hidden out there. Thank you to all the Bobbys of the world.

Posted in Blogs from the book | Leave a reply

Annie looked up at the computer screen once more and then turned towards Narvell, who was sitting on the edge of his bed. "So are you really going to give the company a copy of your blog? I mean … I thought Chris was the only person you let read it. Except me, of course."

"Yeah. I think I will. I've pretty much gotten over the private thing with this one. After all, I didn't write all of this one myself. And I like what Fred said about us using it to guide us on our journey, so we don't forget where we came from.

"And now, Ms. Gerdes, I believe we need to turn off the computer and head on over to Aspen's. Chris and Rob are waiting for us. We've got to get them picked up and get over to Chris' parents for dinner by seven."

"Okay. Okay. But when will all of you know if this has really been a success or not? In other words, when do things get back to normal, or better than normal, at M.E. Burdette Company?" Annie said, shutting down the computer and standing up.

"First of all, I suspect that when things calm down around the engineering changes, we can consider whatever the atmosphere is … that will be the new normal. Hopefully, the progress Jimbo is making and the support he's getting from the entire department will help to get people out of the mode of talking about it all the time. Second, as long as we are seeing progress, we know we are succeeding. I think after about six months of this, though, if the results stay positive, people will feel like we are really succeeding. Then, it's all about sustaining the results … the new culture. Come on, let's go. You can ask Max and Tom about all of this when we get to Tom's house."

***

Narvell still didn't understand how Chris had managed to wind up at Aspen's Lounge without a car. But now that he and Annie had picked up their passengers and driven out to Tom and Sharon Anslemo's house, he decided it really didn't matter. They were here with Rob and Chris to enjoy an evening of food and fellowship with Chris' parents and his grandfather, Max Housholder. Narvell had been thinking on the drive over that it might be nice to not talk shop for once. It seemed to him like every time he had been with Chris, Tom, and Max for the past four-plus months, all they had talked about was the financial situation at M.E. Burdette Co.

Hors d'oeuvres and drinks were followed by dinner, and there was not a single mention of the journey that Narvell, Chris, and M.E. Burdette Co. had been on. Narvell was thrilled. They talked about college days gone by, how Tom and Sharon had met, why and how Max had started Housholder Sprockets, and about Rob's life up in the northeast part of the country. This had truly been a relaxing evening for everyone.

When dessert was served, you could have heard a pin drop, it grew so quiet as everyone was eating the key lime pie Sharon had made. It wasn't until Chris had finished his slice of pie that anyone spoke. Then, Chris looked over at Narvell and asked, "So what's Bobby going to do next fall? Is he enrolling for another semester or what?"

Narvell swallowed a bite of the pie before responding. "Actually, he made the mistake of telling his father about figuring out what Bryan did and that kinda ended his college career. His father informed him that since he was so smart, it was time to start putting that brainpower to use. He's going to work for his father in June."

Everyone got a good laugh out of Narvell's story. As it quieted back down, Max looked over at Chris. "Have you told them yet, my boy?"

Annie's head shot up at Max's question. "Told us what? What's up, Chris?"

"Well … I met with my dad and granddad, and I decided that the best thing I could do to prepare for leadership in Housholder Sprockets was to quit."

"What?" Annie almost shouted. "What are you talking about?"

But before Chris could answer, Narvell was getting in on the questioning. "What in the world are you talking about Chris? Quit what?"

"I'm leaving Housholder Sprockets. I accepted a job with another manufacturer very near to where Rob's office is. I'm moving to the Northeast. I'll have at least one friend when I get there that I can call if it gets tough or lonely. But I really think I need that experience if I want to follow in my father and grandfather's footsteps. I leave next week."

"Wow." That was all Narvell could say. This had really taken him by surprise.

Seeing the surprise on the three youngest people's faces in the room and thinking that it might get awkward very quickly, Sharon jumped in with her usual infectious banter. "And … Annie, how are you and Narvell doing? You've been inseparable for months now. Should I be reserving any weekends this summer?"

And just that quickly the room echoed with laughter.

Narvell finally responded to Sharon. "Mrs. Anselmo, I can assure you that if things get that serious, you will be the first to know." Laughter again. "Actually, right now Annie is too busy trying to get a promotion, and I'm just trying to make sure that everything we've been working on for the past four months continues to get better. This has been a long journey and there is still a long way to go."

Change is the Only Constant

Posted on **January 7, 2012**
Reply

> In our journey to find measurements with meaning, we must remember that the playing field is always changing. That is the only thing that we can be assured of….. Life happens and things change. We MUST continuously evaluate what we measure and how we measure it. Find your tape measure. Don't make it difficult! Enjoy the journey…

—Narvell T. Mann

Posted in Blogs from the book | Leave a reply

Epilogue

The journey is not easy. It is not fast. And, it is never over. Narvell and Chris learned this through their struggles to change the measurement system and the culture at M.E. Burdette Co. But perhaps just as big a lesson was that the journey never ends. Narvell has months, or perhaps even years, of work ahead with Fred in their efforts to create a system of measures that all employees understand and have a sense of ownership in. Likewise, Chris has realized that the growth of any manager or leader does not end simply because one has the position one was seeking. To continue to grow, you must continue to search for ways to improve, whether you are talking about the individual or the organization.

Max Housholder found a way to draw his employees into his vision through personal life experiences of what and how he measured things. Finding your tape measure, whether it is the individual tape measure or that of the whole organization, is the key. You must find out what is important to the organization and measure it in an appropriate manner.

As we stated in the Prologue, You *must* measure the right things. **The things you measure are a reflection of your organizational values. And these values are the fundamental building blocks that shape vision and action. You measure what you value. Measures directly influence how people work. In turn, how people work affects organizational results.** What this means is that an effective measurement system is not just about selecting things to measure. It is about selecting what you value and ensuring that your workforce understands these values. It is not just about measuring; it is also about culture.

Narvell continues to blog from time to time about the lessons he learns concerning not just measures but also leadership and other management principles and philosophies. To follow Narvell's blog, visit Narvell T. Mann— The Tape Measure (http //narvelltmann.wordpress.com). To learn more about the principles used throughout this book, you can visit The Tape Measure Book (www.therightmeasures.com and www.findyourtapemeasure.com).

Just as Narvell's and Chris' journeys continue, we hope your journey to find your tape measure is about to begin!

Appendix

Measurements with Meaning

How to Focus on Success

How Are You Measuring Success Today?

- What measurements are in place currently?

    For the whole company... not just your team
    or department?

- So what about your team / department?

    – How do you measure success at this level?
    – Why?

- How does this benefit the shareholders?

2

What about the Employees?

- Do employees know if the company is successful?
  - How?
  - Which employees?
- Do employees know if they are successful?
  - How?
- Does each employee know how their work specifically impacts the "measurements"?

3

 So Let's Recap M.E. Burdette's Metrics

- Over 300 metrics are on the Big Board by the main break room.
- Who in this room reads the metrics posted?
  - Every single one of them?
  - No? Then which ones?
  - Why?
- Who thinks any employee reads them all?
- Who thinks any employee reads any of them?
- If employees read them, do they know what they mean and how they impact them?

4

So Let's Recap M.E. Burdette's Metrics

- Who knows where the metrics are kept on the network?

- How many of you have looked at them on the network?

- What's the purpose for all these numbers if we can't use them to measure our success and pinpoint our opportunities?

5

Why Are We Here?

- Why does M.E. Burdette Co. exist?
- If the company doesn't make money, how can it survive?
- Then what?
  - What would M.E. Burdette Co.'s employees do?
  - What would you all, the management team, do?
- So, if everyone knows why we are here, who can explain why nearly every department is sub-optimizing?

6

The Dilemma!

What do we do?

Business as usual? Or do we change the model?

7

What Do the Best of the Best Do?

- Apparently we are not the best of the best in town, much less the state, country or industry.

- To be successful, you must always look around you at both success and failure.

- Right here in town we have an example of success.

  – Housholder Sprockets
  – Industry leader, community leader, profitable

8

A Tale of Success

The Tape Measure

9

Time to Start Over

- Create measurements with meaning.
  - Structured from top to bottom within the organization.
  - Everyone in the company MUST know if we are successful or not.

- A few simple measurements at each level of the company can accomplish this.
  - This doesn't mean you don't measure other things.
  - The metrics you post are all linked together.

10

What Success Looks Like

- Start at the top – Key Performance Indicators.
  - Develop 3–4 meaningful KPIs at the top of the organization.
  - Involve stakeholders, managers, and employees alike.
  - Everyone must understand the difference between indicators and goals.
- Top level management MUST be on board ... leading this effort!

11

Success – Top Down

- After KPIs are developed at the top, it's time to start filtering down.
- At the next level down ...
  - Managers must then develop metrics to feed KPIs.
  - These should be objective based and critical to success.
  - There must also be some employee-based metrics that show the employee/team that they are succeeding.
  - Upper-level managers MUST get their team involved to develop the metrics at this level.

12

What Success Looks Like

- Further down the organizational chain:
  - At each level down, management MUST develop metrics that feed upstream towards the KPIs.
  - This is what ties knowledge of success at all levels of the company together.
  - Just as at the higher levels, metrics should be objective based and critical to success.
  - There must also be some employee-based metrics that show the employee/team that they are succeeding.
  - AND, at each level all employees MUST feel ownership in the measurements.
  - Everyone in the organization MUST have their personal success directly linked to meeting these metrics!

13

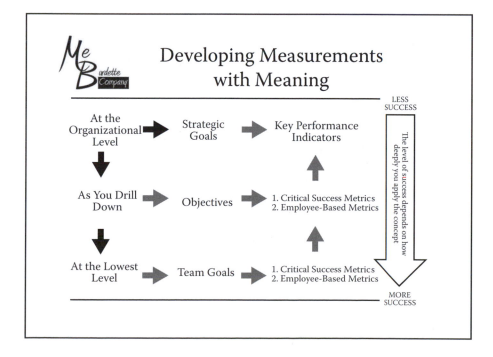

What Success Looks Like

- To truly be successful, employees MUST be engaged!
- Employees have to have ownership in the measurements if you want the effort to succeed culturally.
- There MUST be measurements at each level of the company, from bottom to top, that shows the workforces how they are doing.
- Employees have to be allowed to participate in the creation of some metrics.

15

 Where Do We Start?

- At the top!
  - Name the critical items or areas that should be measured that are critical to our success.
  - Reduce the list to the basic measurements that we MUST know.
  - Convert these to indicators, not goals.
  - How often do we measure them?
- These KPIs will guide us through the rest of our journey.

16

Next Steps

- At each level of the organization repeat the same exercise with these changes:
  - Start by sharing the KPIs and explaining what they are and why they are important to the company's success.
  - Share the critical success metrics from the level above and explain why they are important.
  - Now develop your measurements that support and feed the level above and ultimately feed the KPIs.
  - How often do you measure?
  - Don't forget to create some employee-based metrics that show the team their success!

17

Cultural Sustainment

- Review KPIs annually for relevance.
- After KPI review, start the review process from top to bottom for metrics at each level.
- Celebrate success!
- Learn from Success and Failure!
  - If you fail, determine why! If you succeed, determine why!
  - Sustain the gains (put controls in place and monitor the changes)
  - Communicate results and knowledge obtained
  - Re-evaluate and adjust (if necessary) goals and objectives to meet KPIs

18

The Right Measures Glossary

Actual results – The behavior produced/observed when a component or system is tested

Average – Result obtained by adding together several quantities and then dividing this total by the number of quantities

Average delivery time – Taking multiple delivery times, adding them together and then dividing by the total quantity of times to determine the average.

Blog – A Web site on which an individual or group of users record opinions, information, etc. on a regular basis.

Chart – A sheet of information in the form of a table, graph or diagram

Continuous Improvement – A systematic, proactive approach to assess and improve

Cost analysis -Breaking down the costs of some operation and reporting on each factor separately.

Cost accounting – Cost accounting is the recording and analysis of all the various costs of running a business according to a standardized set of rules or regulations.

Cost calculations – Acomputation to determine the costs or dollars spent associated with each area in a business

Cost effective – Saves or producesa significant amount of money in comparison with the costs involved to run the process from start to finish.

Costing module – The piece of a software system responsible for calculating the cost values of a process or product

Cultural paradigm – People within a culture share the same set of assumptions and similar expectations in how they perceive the world

Cultural sustainment – The ability to retain cultural identity, and to allow change to be guided in ways that are consistent with the cultural values

Current practice – Work procedure which, at present, is accepted as the preferred method for performing a specific task or process

Customer surveys – Customer polling to identify the level of customer satisfaction with an existing product, and to discover the customer's express and hidden needs. This can be achieved through several different methods.

Data – Data are factual information or measures used as a basis for reasoning, discussion, or calculation. The "right" data and its analysis are critical to achieve quality improvement.

Delivery time – Time when actual delivery takes place

Employee information board / metrics board – A physical board (typically a white board) where organizational data are periodically recorded in order to share information (data) for all employees to see

Engineering cost system – The engineering practice or software devoted to project cost management...including technical issues such as the physical design of a structure or system

Enterprise Resource Planning (ERP) – An integrated computer-based system used to manage internal and external resources of a company

Gantt chart – A type of bar chart that illustrates a project schedule/time frame

Goals – A goal is a targeted value of attainment by a design team while building a quality process/product. A goal can also be defined as a customer voice...what the customer is asking for or specifying. Organizational goals can be set by the leadership of an organization in an effort to keep everyone focused on what needs to be achieved.

Graph – A diagram showing the relation between typically two variable quantities, each measured along one of a pair of axes at right angles

Guiding principles – Any principles or precepts that direct or guide an organization throughout its life in all circumstances, irrespective of changes in its goals, strategies, type of work, or the top management.

Indicators – An indicator can be defined as something that helps to understand where you are, where you are going and how far you are from the goal.

Jack Welch, GE – Former CEO of General Electric Company who was credited with GE's turnaround

Jim Collins, *Good to Great* – This book aims to describe how companies transition from being average companies to great companies and how companies can fail to make the transition. "Greatness" is defined as financial performance several multiples better than the market average over a sustained period. Collins finds the main factor for achieving the transition to be a narrow focusing of the company's resources on their field of competence

Key metrics – A type of performance measurement similar to KPIs except that key metrics are commonly found at levels of an organization beneath the top level. See KPIs for additional information.

KPIs/key performance indicators – A type of performance measurement usually found at the highest level of an organization. KPIs are commonly used by an organization to evaluate its overall success or the overall success of a particular activity in which it is engaged. Sometimes success is defined in terms of making progress toward strategic goals, but often success is simply the repeated achievement of some level of operational goal (for example, zero defects, 10/10 customer satisfaction, etc.). Accordingly, choosing the right KPIs is reliant upon having a good understanding of what is important to the organization.

Lean Six Sigma – An integrated methodology, infrastructure and the tools, techniques and skills from Lean and Six Sigma necessary to optimize your processes. Lean focuses on process speed and eliminating waste, while Six Sigma focuses on process quality and eliminating defects and reducing variation in processes.

Lean/Lean manufacturing – Initiative focused on eliminating waste and improving flow in manufacturing processes.

Learning environment – The physical or virtual setting in which learning takes place

Management style – Characteristic ways of making decisions and relating to subordinates

Margins – Company's total sales revenue minus its cost of goods sold, divided by the total sales revenue

Market share – The portion of a market controlled by a particular company or product

Material Resource Planning (MRP) – Computerized ordering and scheduling system for manufacturing and fabrication industries

Mean – The quotient of the sum of several quantities and their number; an average

Measure – Finding a number that shows the size or amount of something

Measurement system – A system of related measures that facilitates the quantification of some particular characteristic

Metric – Parameters or measures of quantitative assessment used for measurement, comparison or to track performance

Optimized – Make the best or most effective use of (a situation, opportunity, or resource).

Organizational culture – The values and behaviors that contribute to the unique social and psychological environment of an organization

Organizational goals and objectives – Goals: Broad spectrum, complex, organizational, indication of program intentions. **Objectives**: Measurable, defined, operational, simple steps, and specific. Objectives contribute to the fulfillment of specified goals. Complete with a beginning and an end.

Organizational learning – Organization-wide continuous process that enhances its collective ability to accept, make sense of, and respond to internal and external change. Organizational learning and is more than the sum of the information held by employees. It requires systematic integration and collective interpretation of new knowledge that leads to collective action and involves risk taking as experimentation.

Organizational measures – Explicit definitions of the characteristics or comparison to criteria (performance, in general) of organizational inputs

Organizational results – The final output that is achieved by an organization

Organizational structure – The framework, typically hierarchical, within which an organization arranges its lines of authority and communications, and allocates rights and duties. Organizational structure determines the manner and extent to which roles, power, and responsibilities are delegated, controlled, and coordinated, and how information flows between levels of management. A structure depends entirely on the organization's objectives and the strategy chosen to achieve them. In a centralized structure, the decision making power is concentrated in the top layer of the management and tight control is exercised over departments and divisions. In a decentralized structure, the decision making power is distributed and the departments and divisions have varying degrees of autonomy. An organizational chart illustrates the organizational structure.

Organizational values – A list (often with an explanation) of the values to which the organization subscribes. The document reflects the approach the organization takes to its publics, provides insight on its world view, and helps define and direct its commitment to corporate social responsibility

Overhead dollars – Resources consumed or lost in completing a process that does not contribute directly to the end-product. The ongoing administrative expenses of a business which cannot be attributed to any specific business activity, but are still necessary for the business to function. Examples include rent, utilities, and insurance.

Performance indicators – Defined set of values used to measure against

Peter Senge, *The Fifth Discipline: The Art and Practice of the Learning Organization* – Based on fifteen years of experience in putting the book's ideas into practice. Senge makes clear that in the long run the only sustainable competitive advantage is your organization's ability to learn faster than the competition. The leadership stories in the book demonstrate the many ways that the core ideas in *The Fifth Discipline*, many of which seemed radical when first published in 1990, have become deeply integrated into people's ways of seeing the world and their managerial practices.

Profit – A financial benefit that is realized when the amount of revenue gained from a business activity exceeds the expenses, costs and taxesneeded to sustain the activity

Quality – Continuous and dynamic adaptation of products and services to fulfill or exceed the requirements or expectations of all parties in the organization, the customer, industry and the community as a whole

Range – The area of variation between upper and lower limits on a particular scale.

Root cause – An initiating cause of a causal chain which leads to an outcome or effect of interest

Six Sigma – A strategy-driven, process-focused, project-enabled organizational improvement initiative. The goal of Six Sigma is to increase profits by reducing variability and defects that undermines customer loyalty...leading to bottom-line profitability and top-line growth. Six Sigma is a methodology that provides businesses with the tools to improve the capability of their business processes. This increase in performance and decrease in process variation leads to defect reduction and vast improvement in profits, employee morale and quality of product. Six Sigma focuses on process quality.

Strategic business unit (SBU) – a business unit within the overall corporate identity which is distinguishable from other business because it serves a defined external market where management can conduct strategic planning in relation to products and markets

Strategic Planning – A disciplined effort to produce fundamental decisions and actions that shape and guide what an organization is, what it does, and why it does it, with a focus on the future. Determines the strategic goals and objectives of the organization, short and long term.

Sub-optimized – Situation where a process, procedure, or system yields less than the best possible outcome or output, caused by a lack of best possible coordination between different components, elements, parts, etc.

Task – A piece of work to be done or undertaken

Team goals – The result or achievement toward which effort is directed by a group of people

Team member – A person belonging to a specific group of people involved in attempting to achieve a common goal

Teamwork – The combined action of a group of people, especially focused on effectiveness and efficiency

Theory X vs. Theory Y – **Theory X** states that some people have an inherent dislike for work and will avoid it whenever. These people need to be controlled and coerced by their managers to achieve production. **Theory Y** states that some people see work as natural and will be self-directing if they are committed to the objectives. The manager's role with these people is to help them achieve their potential.

Unit Cost – The amount of money that it costs a company to produce one article, or piece, of work

Value – Value is the exchange for which a customer pays. A product or service's capability provided to a customer at the right time, at an appropriate price, as defined in each case by the customer.

Value-added – To be a value-added action, the action must meet all three of the following criteria:
1) The customer is willing to pay for this activity.
2) It must be done right the first time.
3) The action must somehow change the product or service in some positive manner.

Vision – A series of brief sentences of paragraphs that describes the "big goals" that your business hopes to achieve over time. It can also present the heights you believe your business may reach and what you want your business to be after a certain period of time. Describes a desirable state that a company wishes to attain at some time in the future

Voice of the Customer (VOC) – Describes the stated and unstated needs or requirements of the customer. The voice of the customer can be captured in a variety of ways: Direct discussion or interviews, surveys, focus groups, customer specifications, observation, warranty data, field reports, complaint logs, etc.

Voice of the Process (VOP) – Term used to describe what the process is telling you. What it is capable of achieving, whether it is predictable or unpredictable and what significance to attach to individual measurements. The key is to align the Voice of the Process to the Voice of Customer.

About the Authors

Mark A. Nash is Operations Manager for Pelco Products, Inc. He has over 25 years of process improvement experience, both as an internal and external consultant/engineer, in manufacturing, distribution, government, and healthcare. This diversified background allows Nash to work outside the box looking for process solutions many people cannot visualize.

A multiskilled Six Sigma Black Belt, Nash is also a certified NIST/MEP Lean Master trainer, having partnered with the Oklahoma Manufacturing Alliance to provide Lean manufacturing training throughout the state of Oklahoma. Nash has facilitated more than 400 Lean workshops and has facilitated kaizen events for more than 50 organizations worldwide. He is a senior member of the American Society for Quality, and is a senior member of the Institute of Industrial Engineers.

During his time at Pelco Products, the company has been recognized numerous times for their Lean efforts including *Quality Magazine's* presentation of the 2010 Quality Plant of the Year Award, and being named a 2011 Lean Best Practice Finalist by the Institute of Industrial Engineers.

Prior to joining the Pelco team, Nash served as a managing director for an international process engineering firm. Nash was a member of Iomega Corporation's process improvement team, which was named a finalist in the large manufacturer category of the 2000 RIT/USA Today Quality Cup competition. He has presented at numerous conferences around the world including the ASQ Six Sigma, IIE Lean Management Solutions, American Association for Clinical Chemistry, Frontiers in Laboratory Medicine Association for Manufacturing

Excellence and Lab Quality Confab. Additionally, Nash served as an advisor to the University of Central Oklahoma's Center for Strategic Improvement.

Nash is a contributing columnist to *Quality Magazine*, and has been published in *IE Industrial Engineer* magazine and *The Bulletin of the Royal College of Pathologists* (United Kingdom). He is a coauthor of the 2006 Productivity Press book, *Using Lean for Faster Six Sigma Results: A Synchronized Approach*, and is a coauthor of the 2008 Productivity Press book, *Mapping the Total Value Stream: A Comprehensive Guide to Production and Transactional Processes*.

Sheila R. Poling is a Managing Partner and Owner of Pinnacle Partners, Inc. With more than 25 years' experience in the quality and productivity industry, she previously served as vice president of two nationally recognized consulting/training firms and a book publishing firm. Her management responsibilities have included managing over 35 consultants and administrative staff. Poling's broad professional experience includes work in operations management, product, training materials and seminar development, marketing and sales, client interface, and customer satisfaction initiatives focused on business excellence with an emphasis on leadership and quality.

A prolific writer, Poling has coauthored several books, including the internationally recognized *Customer Focused Quality*, a book on customer satisfaction and service, and *Building Continual Improvement: SPC for the Service Industry and Administrative Areas*. She has served as a primary editor for a featured monthly column in *Quality* magazine and is coauthor of *Brain Teasers: Real-World Challenges to Build Your Manufacturing Skills*, published by *Quality*. McGraw-Hill's *The Manufacturing Engineering Handbook*, released in 2004, features her chapter on "Six Sigma and Lean Implementation." She is a contributing columnist to *Quality Magazine* and is coauthor of the 2006 Productivity Press release, *Using Lean for Faster Six Sigma Results: A Synchronized Approach*, and the 2008 Productivity Press release, *Mapping the Total Value Stream: A Comprehensive Guide for Production and Transactional Processes*.

Poling has also coauthored several work manuals, including "Perfecting Continual Improvement Skills" and "Strategy-Driven Six Sigma: A Champion

Overview." In addition, she has helped design multiple course offerings focused on leadership training, organizational and operations excellence, Six Sigma, Lean, and statistical process control. She is currently serving on the American Society for Quality's Six Sigma Committee and on the Innovation Research Committee.

Poling holds a degree in Business Administration from the University of Tennessee and is a Fellow of the American Society for Quality as well as a member of the American Marketing Association and American Management Association. She has also had the privilege to study and work closely with many distinguished industry leaders, including W. Edwards Deming.